Focused Early Learning

→ A Planning Framework for Teaching Young Children

Gaye Gronlund

Redleaf Press
St. Paul, Minnesota
www.redleafpress.org

© 2003 Gaye Gronlund
All rights reserved.

Published by: Redleaf Press
                a division of Resources for Child Caring
                450 N. Syndicate, Suite 5
                St. Paul, MN 55104

Visit us online at www.redleafpress.org

Library of Congress Cataloging-in-Publication Data

Gronlund, Gaye, 1952–
    Focused early learning : a planning framework for teaching young children / Gaye Gronlund.
        p. cm.
    Includes bibliographical references and index.
    ISBN 1-929610-30-0 (pbk.)
    1. Early childhood education—United States—Curricula.
2. Active learning—United States. I. Title.
LB1139.4.G76 2003
372.21—dc21

2002155342

To preschool teachers everywhere. I salute you for the work you do with children and families.

To my own family. Thank you for the love and support we share.

Acknowledgments

Thank you to the following teachers who tried out the frameworks, gave feedback, and shared their plans:

- Diana Lamb
- Pam Giermann
- Vicki Bruno
- Mary Schumacher-Hoerner
- Valerie Bylina
- Veronica Cisowski
- Gerlinde Janowski

And thank you to my editor, Beth Wallace, whose comments always add clarity to my writing and thinking.

Contents

Introduction **vii**

Chapter 1 Preschool Curriculum **1**

Chapter 2 The Focused Early Learning Frameworks **11**

Chapter 3 Creating a Rich Classroom Environment **25**

Chapter 4 Developing Relationships with Children and Families **43**

Chapter 5 Academic and Developmental Learning Activities **57**

Chapter 6 Physical Energy Outlets and Outdoor Explorations **69**

Chapter 7 Balancing Child Choice with Teacher-Led Activities **81**

Chapter 8 Following Children's Interests with Ongoing Projects/Studies **97**

Chapter 9 Focused Observations and Assessing Children's Learning **117**

Appendix A Focused Early Learning Forms **147**

Appendix B References **159**

Index **160**

Introduction

I wrote this book as a result of my own teaching and consulting experiences. I have taught in a variety of settings around the country: a cooperative nursery school, a university lab school, Head Start, special education preschools, and kindergarten. As a college instructor and early childhood education consultant, I have worked with thousands of teachers around the country, helping them to identify the best ways to implement recommended curricular strategies and meet the needs of the children in their unique settings.

In my work, teachers often raise concerns about planning for active learning environments. They can see positive results in arranging their classrooms to facilitate children's engagement. They recognize the value of giving children choices. They see the need to plan activities that can address a range of individual children's abilities. But, preschool teachers ask questions such as the following:

- "How do I do all of this?"
- "How do I give children choices and not have absolute chaos?"
- "Is it okay to plan teacher-directed activities?"
- "How do I write a lesson plan for exploration?"
- "How do I show the ways that I followed the children's interests and changed activities and materials in the classroom?"

The question I hear most frequently is

- "How do I record everything that I'm doing, to be child-focused and responsive, to integrate all of what I know are best practices, into some sort of lesson plan?"

This book is my attempt to answer these questions.

The Focused Early Learning Frameworks

Teachers of preschool children often combine a variety of curricular approaches and strategies that fall under the general heading of "developmentally appropriate practices." They incorporate aspects of environment-based learning centers with curriculum that emerges from children's interests. They integrate academic learning into hands-on exploration and pay very close attention to children's social and emotional development as well.

When combining such approaches, however, teachers have had to figure out how to record their plans. They have not had an outline for planning, nor a record of the actual happenings in the classroom as they responded to children's interests and enthusiasms.

This book will present two kinds of frameworks: one for planning and the other for reflection. These frameworks will help teachers "pull it all together" and represent the integration of the very best curricular approaches they are using every day in the classroom.

Preschool children have needs and learning traits that influence classroom planning and curriculum. The frameworks in this book are designed to help teachers organize the classroom and plan activities that will work with the needs and traits of this age group, rather than against them.

This process for planning encompasses the incredible number of accommodations and details in the life of a successful preschool classroom. This process will help teachers develop an ongoing record of the ways that they integrate their own knowledge of child development with the specific needs and interests of the children they teach. This record can then become a tool for planning and reflection, as well as for supervision and communication with families.

In addition, each section of the book will focus on certain aspects of teaching preschool children. Recognizing that there are many fine curricular approaches that have been developed for preschool classrooms (such as the Creative Curriculum, the High/Scope curriculum, the Project Approach, emergent curriculum, and the Reggio approach), this book will not attempt to reinvent the wheel. Instead, it will offer ways to integrate the best of these approaches into a cohesive whole with the planning and reflection frameworks providing the structure.

Field-Testing the Frameworks

Several teachers graciously agreed to try out the Focused Early Learning Frameworks in their classrooms. This is very important to me. I never want to make suggestions that are not based in real everyday classroom life. Therefore, I am deeply grateful to my colleagues who have willingly used the frameworks so that they could be "tried and tested."

Five teachers in particular have shared their experiences with the frameworks with me. They represent a variety of programs around the country. All have extensive experience working with young children, and all were willing to give me honest, constructive feedback. Their comments will be included throughout the book so that you can hear from practitioners in action.

Let me tell you a little about each one of them.

Diana Lamb is the owner and teacher at Little Lambs Nursery School in Lebanon, Indiana. She is also a tirelessly dedicated member of her local AEYC (Association for the Education of Young Children) and her county Step Ahead Council, and she is a Child Development Associate (CDA) instructor. Diana's program is truly unusual. Set on a working farm owned by Diana and her husband, the program includes regular visits to the sheep and cow barn and the chicken coop. Lately, Diana has been considering retirement from preschool—however, her community is forever enthusiastically persuading her to continue providing her quality program in this rural area that has very few alternatives.

Pam Giermann is an early childhood educator for the West Chicago Public Schools. Her classroom includes young children with special needs integrated with those identified as at-risk and with local community children whose parents pay tuition. Pam has taught for years and often has student teachers placed in her classroom. She is pursuing her master's degree and conducts workshops for other teachers in her spare time.

Vicki Bruno is a special education teacher for the Central Consolidated Schools located on the Navajo Reservation in Shiprock, New Mexico. Her caseload includes ten children with a variety of identified special needs. Vicki is vice president of New Mexico AEYC and a tireless advocate for children.

Mary Schumacher-Hoerner is also a preschool teacher at Central Consolidated. Her students are identified as at-risk through a state-funded program. Both Vicki and Mary have extensive experience working with Navajo children and families.

Valerie Bylina is a preschool special educator with the Sandridge School District in Lynwood, Illinois. Her children are three-, four-, and five-year-olds with a variety of special needs including speech and language delays, borderline autism, and behavior disorders. Valerie has been trained to be a mentor teacher and mentors her new assistants and the new kindergarten teachers. She has also taken the lead in her district to implement the new Illinois Early Learning Standards in her curriculum and assessment practices.

In addition to the teachers named above, Veronica Cisowski and Gerlinde Janowski of the West Chicago Community School District shared some of their early experiments with the lesson-planning framework. I am grateful to them, and to all of the teachers who have contributed to the writing of this book.

chapter 1

The Focused Early Learning Weekly Planning Framework

Date:_____ Teacher:_____

Child-led Exploration in the Rich Classroom Environment

- Blocks
- Dramatic Play
- Manipulatives
- Art
- Ongoing Projects
- Math Moments
- Reading and Writing
- Sensory Table
- Library
- Writing Center
- Scientific Inquiries

Individual Adjustments

Steps to Relationship Building

Preschool Curriculum

The Focused Early Learning Frameworks will help teachers integrate all the planning and accommodating that they are already doing. But what are the frameworks based on? In this chapter we'll talk about the key components of a good preschool curriculum, which have been identified from my experiences as a classroom teacher, and my journey as a consultant and coach alongside other preschool teachers. Many of them will look familiar to you because some of these factors are discussed in every good preschool curriculum approach.

In each section, I'll define the component and talk about what it means in the classroom and why it's important. Then I'll refer you to the chapter in the book where this component is discussed specifically in reference to the frameworks. The frameworks are built around these components—they are at the heart of day-to-day implementation of the frameworks with children in the classroom.

Five Key Components of Quality Preschool Curriculum

1. *Learning*—Learning is at the core of the preschool curriculum—whether learning about the weather, the alphabet, hand washing, or how to get along with twenty other children. At all times, teachers keep in mind learning goals that will support the healthy development of each child.

2. *A Rich Classroom Environment*—The classroom environment is the most important source for learning activities and must be organized and used in ways that make learning positive, engaging, active, and exciting.

3. *Respectful, Caring Relationships*—Teachers and children build strong, caring relationships through their daily interactions. Teachers get to know each child well. Children learn to trust and take risks because of the respect and caring their teachers give them.

4. *Observation and Reflection*—Teachers carefully observe children in action, noticing what they are interested in, what they like and dislike, what is hard or easy for them to do. Teachers assess children's development formally and informally, thinking carefully about what the next step might be for each child. At the same time, they reflect on what happens each day in the classroom: what worked, what didn't work, what proved especially engaging for children, where children might be bored or restless. They assess their own planning and preparation.

5. *Adjustments and Accommodations*—Based on their observations and reflections, teachers make adjustments and accommodations in the curriculum to support the learning of individual children and of the group. To help children be successful, teachers make changes both spontaneously and after thoughtful planning. It is important to evaluate the following areas:
   - Available materials
   - Activity length
   - Level of physical involvement (active or passive)
   - Amount of teacher direction versus the amount of child choice
   - Activity themes (teacher-determined or based on children's interests)
   - Activity goals or goals for individual children

Key Component 1: Learning

Collectively, the frameworks in this book are called "Focused Early Learning" to keep this first key component clearly at the forefront of our thinking. More and more concern is being voiced in the media and heard from community members, parents, and governmental agencies that schooling must help children rise to higher educational standards. Such concerns are now turning toward preschool programs throughout the country.

In an editorial published on October 20, 2000, the editors of *USA Today* raised concerns that many programs for young children offer merely "pablum" learning opportunities, rather than "rigorous academics." Their comments were in reference to the fact that the presidential candidates at the time were urging us to expect all children to read by the third grade. The editors said, "Why wait that long?" They recommended that children attend "academically rigorous preschools to get advanced reading, math and fine motor skills." Throughout the editorial they endorsed preschools that "push" academic skills—especially the ability to recognize letters and identify beginning sounds of words. They praised programs that were "carrying out aggressive early reading programs." I hear lots of words that concern me in this editorial: *rigorous, push, aggressive.* Do those words concern you?

What's wrong with this picture? In its signature document defining the best practices for young children, the National Association for the Education of Young Children (NAEYC) cautions against inappropriate expectations for young children. Are academics an inappropriate expectation?

The critical answer to this question involves how those academics are presented to children. All developmentally appropriate programs should include stimulating learning opportunities for children in a variety of content areas. Teachers should be accountable for the skills and concepts young children gain in their classrooms. However, children should not be relegated to being passive, with teachers acting as instructors, imparting knowledge to "empty vessels." Instead, children should actively learn academics, with teachers acting as facilitators and guides more than instructors.

Quality programs for children three to five years of age *are* academic programs. They include carefully planned opportunities for children to rigorously learn more about the world around them, to develop skills and competencies, to understand concepts, and to gain knowledge. The academics of these programs are carefully imbedded in the active learning environment. Situations are planned so those children can figure things out for themselves. They are exposed to new materials and possibilities. They are supported and challenged by teachers who know the best ways to match learning activities to the traits of this age group.

When teachers incorporate academics into the curriculum, they are raising the level of accountability. By writing clear goals in the planning framework, teachers are reminding themselves and communicating to others that indeed they are thinking first and foremost about learning. Teachers are helping others witness how much they know about their children's growth and development and how hard they are working to support and challenge each child.

In chapters 3, 5, and 9, we will explore ways you can use the frameworks to document this attention to learning goals.

Key Component 2: A Rich Classroom Environment

The room arrangement and presentation of materials communicate important messages to the children. Those messages deeply affect behavior. If the classroom is messy and disorganized, children will probably not take good care of the materials. If the shelves are placed along the walls so that huge open spaces dominate the room, children may run and jump, actions much more suitable for outdoors. On the other hand, if materials are carefully organized and presented in a clear, appealing fashion, children may treat them with more care and put them away more easily at clean-up time. If shelving and tables are used to create specific learning areas throughout the room and placed in a way that breaks up running paths and creates intimate spaces for using certain materials, children will settle down and become engaged with activities for longer periods of time and with more productive ends.

When the environment is functioning as a key part of the preschool curriculum, the room arrangement literally directs children toward the productive use of materials in specific areas. Noise levels are considered so that materials that tend toward greater physical and verbal involvement on the part of the children are placed near each other. Materials that tend toward quieter use are also grouped near each other.

In chapter 3, we will explore ways to use the frameworks to plan for the most effective use of the classroom environment. In chapters 7 and 8, we will discuss ways to balance children's choices with teacher-led activities so that children's productive exploration of the classroom can take place without chaos or anarchy.

Key Component 3: Respectful, Caring Relationships

The classroom environment is the centerpiece of good early childhood curriculum because it allows young children to be active explorers, yet provides structure and guidance for their exploration. Being an explorer means being a risk-taker. However, young children will not take risks in a classroom unless they feel safe and trusting. They turn to the adults in the environment to provide that safety, and to earn their trust. When they establish a caring relationship with those adults, they will venture further, develop more independence, try new activities, and experiment with new peer relationships.

Building relationships with children is an ongoing task involving observation, intuition, and knowledge of age-appropriate behaviors and skills. It also involves getting to know each child's family—asking questions about the cultural background, the members of the household, and the family's dreams and goals for the child can help teachers work together with family members to support the child more fully.

We will discuss in more detail ways to get to know each child well and incorporate that knowledge into the frameworks in chapters 4 and 9.

Key Component 4: Observation and Reflection

Teachers watch the children in their care all the time. They listen carefully to their words. They read their body language. They note their emotional tone. They see the lightbulb going on when a child understands a new concept or masters a new skill. They recognize frustration when a child has difficulty with something or someone.

Teachers are constantly observing the children in their classroom. Ms. Anne sees Joey trying to cut with scissors. As he turns them upside down, she notes his growing frustration and spontaneously decides to move toward him and offer assistance. She carefully places her hand over his, turns his hand upside down, and helps him to make a snip. He smiles broadly. "You did it!" she says.

Quiet, reflective time to think carefully about what's happening with each and every child is also necessary to be a good preschool teacher. Replaying in our brains the videotape of the day, reviewing observation notes, thinking back over those exciting teachable moments that worked, and those activities that didn't, are essential to providing quality early childhood education. Often in reflection teachers adjust lesson plans, consider individual children's needs, evaluate the way they handled a difficult behavior, or rethink classroom arrangement. Throughout the remaining chapters, teachers' actual reflections will illustrate how best to implement the frameworks to help with this important process.

Key Component 5: Adjustments and Accommodations

Preschool teachers make hundreds of spontaneous decisions each day—they cut the story short because they see the wiggles coming out in the group or they decide to read another story because the children are so attentive. They pull out a set of materials or a piece of equipment on the spur of the moment to accommodate a child's deep interest, or her need for physical motion on a day too rainy to go outside.

Preschool teachers also make hundreds of planned accommodations to help children learn or to build relationships. They seat certain children next to each other because they recognize that will be successful. Or they seat a child on their own lap for just the same reason. They plan a change to the manipulative area because they notice that the puzzles are not being cared for, and they hypothesize that the available puzzles are too easy for many of the children.

Whether spontaneous or carefully planned, all of these adjustments and accommodations are based on careful observation and deep knowledge of the children, and thoughtful reflection about the daily happenings in the classroom. Here are the main categories in which teachers make these changes:

Available Materials

Changing the materials that are available in the classroom is a curricular decision. A teacher carefully plans the basic environment. She recognizes the importance of communicating order, structure, and extensive possibilities for the productive use of materials. Evaluating the classroom environment is a continual job. A teacher must ask: "How effectively is the set up contributing to the children's comfort, risk taking, and learning?" The environment must be changed only to make it more effective in these ways.

In chapter 3, we will give many sample plans using the framework to demonstrate how teachers determine when changes are needed and what those changes should be.

Activity Length

The length of activities, as well as the flow from one activity to another, is an important accommodation point in a preschool classroom. Looking carefully at the daily schedule and considering the needs of the children is essential. Knowing when to end an activity because the children are no longer engaged, or when to extend an activity because their interest is high, is important for effective preschool teaching. In chapter 7, we'll look at time as a factor in planning and implementing the preschool curriculum.

Level of Physical Involvement

The level of physical involvement in activities is another important consideration. Whether it is circle time or large group time, which is usually led by the teacher, or choice time with the children choosing the activities, determining how active or passive the children's involvement will be greatly influences the general sense of organization and calm of the classroom.

Young children are physical and active. They need many outlets for their energy and emotional expressions. Preschool teachers know this very well. And, they know that a brief recess or outdoor time will not provide enough release to meet children's needs. Therefore, they make sure that the classroom environment provides opportunities for movement, exploration, and hands-on manipulation of objects. They carefully evaluate their daily schedule to make sure that sitting and listening times are briefer than times for hands-on activities.

In chapter 6, we'll explore ways to include physical energy outlets for children both indoors and out. In chapter 7, I will introduce some ideas about determining how to balance physical involvement in large and small group times and how to note that on the frameworks.

Amount of Teacher Direction Versus the Amount of Child Choice

Determining when activities should be teacher-directed and when they should be the result of the children's choices is another important balancing act in preschool classrooms. Teachers recognize that offering choices leads to more participation and engagement in activities. In chapter 7, we will explore this balance in depth and apply it to the planning framework.

Activity Themes

The focus of activities can be decided by the teachers, or it can be chosen by the children, who have shown a strong interest. This is another way to provide choices for the children. There are many curricular approaches that suggest specific ways to go about planning with the children's interests in mind. These approaches include the Project Approach, emergent curriculum, and the Reggio approach (based on the curricular practices at the schools for young children in Reggio Emilia, Italy). Sensitive and responsive teachers have always recognized the interests of the children in their classroom and incorporated activities spontaneously or in a carefully planned manner.

Again, this is a balancing act on the teacher's part. Curricular themes do not need to be only child-determined. Nor should they be only teacher-generated. In chapter 8, we will explore this balancing act in depth. In chapters 3 and 8, there are several examples of the ways the teachers used the frameworks to show their teacher- and child-initiated themes.

Activity Goals or Goals for Individual Children

Identifying developmental goals for specific activities or for specific children is at the heart of an individualized preschool curriculum with learning as its primary purpose. The goals chosen by a teacher do not come out of thin air. Instead, they are carefully considered and reflect the best thinking about child development from the early childhood education field. Teachers can turn to one of the many developmental checklists or milestones charts available and use them as the source for goal setting on the planning framework.

Deciding on specific goals for activities or individual children is an ongoing process that happens through observational assessment in the classroom, and reflection and thinking after the preschool day has ended. By combining the planning and the reflection process, the teachers are more cognizant of the children's needs. There is a connection from week to week that builds on the children's interests and capabilities. Assessment information gained through observing the children is integrated into planning for the next set of activities. The curriculum flows more smoothly.

Throughout the chapters of this book, we will look at the combination of planning and reflection and goal setting. And, in chapter 9, we will consider focused observations and authentic assessment processes.

How to Use This Book

The following chapters are set up to highlight and focus on specific sections of the planning and reflection frameworks. In chapter 2, the complete frameworks are introduced to give you the big picture. Each subsequent chapter has a section of the framework and specific suggestions and examples of how to use it in the planning and reflection processes. Each chapter ends with a discussion of how to implement the key curricular components. These discussion sections are called "Focus on Teaching."

chapter 2

The Focused Early Learning Weekly Planning Framework

Date:_____ Teacher:_____

Child-led Exploration in the Rich Classroom Environment

- Art
- Sensory Table
- Library
- Blocks
- Writing Center
- Dramatic Play
- Ongoing Projects
- Manipulatives
- Scientific Inquiries
- Math Moments
- Reading and Writing
- Individual Adjustments
- Steps to Relationship Building

The Focused Early Learning Frameworks

The design of both the planning and the reflection frameworks attempts to include as many of the recommended teaching approaches from high-quality early childhood curricula as possible. There are a variety of labeled boxes where teachers can write plans and later, there are reflections about the plans' results. Dividing the planning task into these specific areas allows teachers to keep track of the many ways they engage young children, support their learning, build trust and friendship with them, and continually challenge them to their fullest potential.

The boxes on the framework include the following:

- Child-Led Exploration in the Rich Classroom Environment (with learning areas identified as Blocks, Art, Sensory Table, Dramatic Play, Library, Manipulatives, and Writing Center)
- Ongoing Projects
- Steps to Relationship Building
- Individual Adjustments
- Reading and Writing
- Math Moments
- Scientific Inquiries
- Physical Energy Outlets
- Outdoor Explorations
- Focused Observations
- Challenging Children's Thinking
- Teacher-Led Large Group
- Teacher-Led Small Group

The Focused Early Learning Framework has two very similar sheets to be filled out by teachers at two different times, one for planning and one for reflection. *(Photocopy-ready framework sheets can be found in the appendix.)*

The Planning Framework

The planning framework is designed to be used by teachers when thinking ahead to the next week in their classroom. It gives focus to the use of the environment and any changes to be made to it. It helps a teacher organize necessary materials ahead of time, as well as consider special activities such as stories, songs, finger plays, science experiments, or project activities. It also reminds a teacher to make individual adjustments or conduct focused observations.

Most of the boxes are meant to be completed on a weekly basis. Young children do not need the whole classroom environment and choice of activities to change every day. They appreciate the opportunity to try things again and again, practicing and refining their skills and knowledge, and learning to deepen their involvement with various materials. In chapter 3, we will explore more fully when to consider changing materials and activities to meet the needs of the children and to enrich the curriculum.

Only the teacher-led groups (both large and small) are listed so that daily plans can be written. Teachers often do change the storybooks they read each day, or the songs and finger plays they sing and chant. Goals for

> **Vicki:** *"It pulls everything together and gives you a format. The framework helps you see that you are including all the different areas of development throughout your classroom activities. So many teachers are using so many different resources and pulling from each one, resources like The Mailbox® and books. The Focused Early Learning Framework is a terrific way to see it all together."*

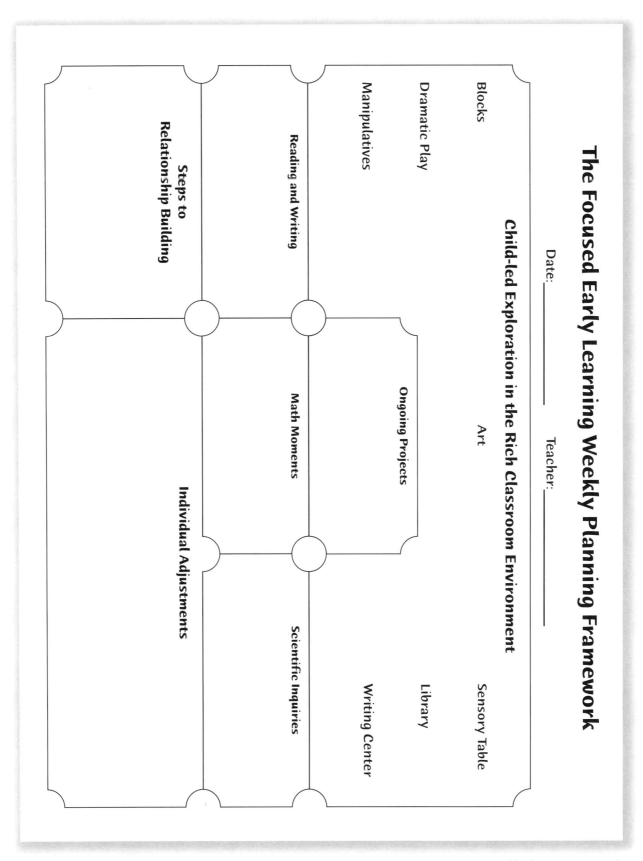

Weekly Planning Framework

Outdoor Explorations

Challenging Children's Thinking

Physical Energy Outlets

Focused Observations

	Monday	Tuesday	Wednesday	Thursday	Friday
Teacher-led Large Group Activities					
Teacher-led Small Group Activities					

small group times can also change daily, if desired. The framework lists the five days of the week, then, for these group times.

You can see that the framework has the basic classroom environment as its centerpiece. In addition, it offers guidelines for making changes in that environment—changes that may be related to specific academic content areas such as math, reading/writing, or science, as well as changes that may challenge the children's thinking or incorporate their ideas and interests into projects or long-term studies. It also recognizes the need for young children to be active and use their extensive physical energy within that environment.

But the environment is meaningless without the people who function in it day in and day out. Teachers facilitate children's use of the environment. In order to do so, they first build trusting, caring relationships with children. They express their faith in children's potential and their willingness to help them to grow and learn. They then offer a wide range of opportunities within the environment. Some of those opportunities allow children to make choices, to follow their own or their peers' interests. Some of those opportunities are adult-led or adult-chosen. A careful balance with flexibility for individual differences is all-important.

Building relationships with young children includes building relationships with their families. Children do not arrive at early childhood programs in a vacuum. They arrive with life experiences within their own family unit, influenced by the cultural backgrounds and values of their family members. Teachers recognize that continually working on ways to know and understand more about each child includes learning more about the child's family. Communication and open-and-welcoming policies are essential to quality programs.

The planning framework incorporates ways for teachers to include their relationship-building steps with the children while in the planning process. It includes recording individual adjustments within the curriculum as teachers learn more about each child's strengths, developmental challenges, and individual characteristics. And, the framework contains a way of observing the children so individual adjustments can be made.

The Reflection Framework

Teachers are very busy people. Their jobs demand that they be "on" whenever the children are present. Quiet, reflective time does not occur very often when twenty three- and four-year-olds are active and engaged. Yet, taking time to think about ways to work with individual children is essential. By

Diana: *"I really didn't think I was interested in any more paperwork. So, I thought it looked good but I set it aside. After a while, I started thinking about it, and came back to the organized format again and again, saying to myself, 'This is what I already do! It's all right here!' Now, I'm using it and finding that having this kind of record is more comprehensive than my earlier lesson planning."*

Valerie: *"This lesson plan format is great! I like putting all of the activities down in one place. I used to be all over the place and others couldn't make sense of exactly what I was doing."*

> **Mary:** *"I'm enjoying the format as both a plan and a map, as an ongoing record of activities, and as a record to demonstrate all that we do each day. It helps show that during our play, for instance, there is learning going on and that important concepts are being introduced and experienced."*

> **Vicki:** *"This framework will be so helpful to beginning teachers. This is what's engrained in my head. And, even I sometimes will forget! This way, I can pull it all together."*

including reflection as an important part of the planning process, I hope to demonstrate to teachers, supervisors, and outsiders how important reflection is to good preschool teaching.

The framework includes two possibilities for formalizing the reflection process so it becomes a written document of importance. The first possibility, the reflection framework, looks almost exactly the same as the planning framework. However, its purpose is completely different. Here is a tool for teachers to record the actual occurrences in their classroom as they implement the plan written on the framework. As the week progresses, day-to-day reflections about ways the children used the materials provided, or responded to specific activities, can be recorded.

This reflection sheet contains the same labeled boxes that the planning framework has. In the boxes, teachers can make notes about what worked and didn't work in their weekly plan. They can write down individual children's responses to activities or difficulties with concepts. They can keep a record of spontaneous changes the teaching team may have made in the room arrangement or of planned events as the week went on. They can jot down ideas for possible new activities for the next week from ideas that were generated by the children. They can give themselves written reminders to keep specific materials available in the next week or to make sure to include something in the next plan.

When using the reflection sheet, it is not necessary to fill in every single box (as was done in the planning process). Instead, record significant thoughts in the appropriate boxes. If the materials and choices in the various learning areas worked well, you may just note a smiling face in that section of the form. However, if you observed that very few children chose to go to one of those learning areas, note that. Or, if the children brought new materials to the dramatic play area and changed the focus of their interactions there from keeping house to acting out the roles for a stuffed animals' hospital, note that as well. Then, next week's plan will build on the children's interest, perhaps by changing that area into a veterinarian's office.

Important Areas for Reflection

Some areas should get attention each week on the reflection framework because they involve individual children and help to correlate your curriculum with those children's needs. The following areas should be a focus for reflection each week: steps to relationship building, individual adjustments, and focused observations.

Some areas on the reflection form help to determine how children are learning various concepts and skills. Noting the successes of children in

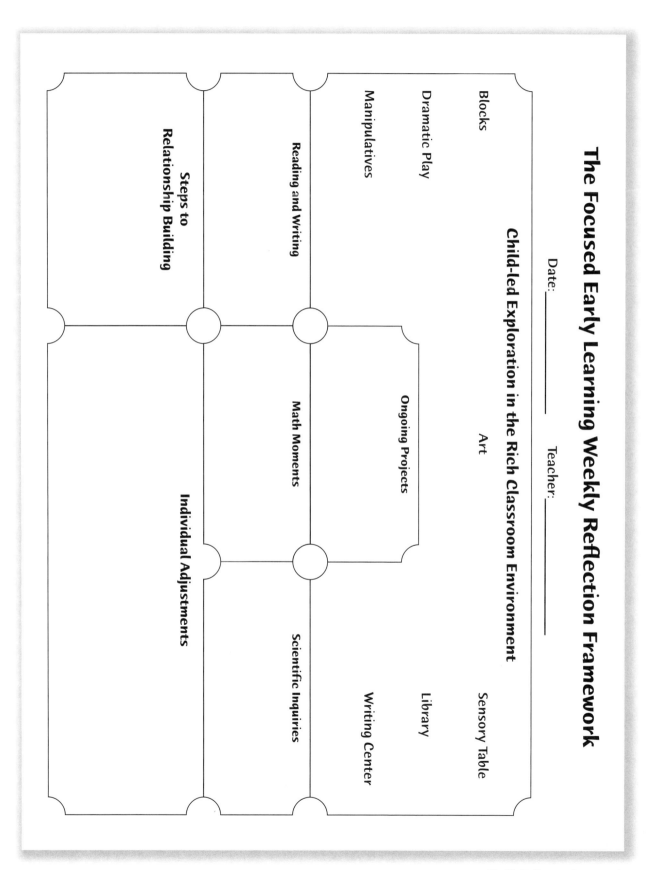

Weekly Reflection Framework

Weekly Reflection Framework

Physical Energy Outlets / **Outdoor Explorations**

Focused Observations / **Challenging Children's Thinking**

	Monday	Tuesday	Wednesday	Thursday	Friday
Teacher-led Large Group Activities					
Teacher-led Small Group Activities					

the more academic areas of reading/writing, math, and scientific inquiries will help you determine what activities to offer next. Are the children ready for greater challenges in these subject areas? Or do they need more time to practice specific skills or explore certain concepts? In addition, noting the results of activities coordinated with an ongoing project or study can help determine the next steps in continuing children's engagement with that project.

General Reflection Sheet

The second possibility for recording this important process is a more general reflection form, which includes four basic categories where you can jot notes: what worked well, what did not work well, individual child information, to consider in future plans. Some teachers have suggested that having the two forms so similar was confusing and overwhelming. This general form can be used to note the same types of information as listed above but in a more streamlined manner.

When to Use the Reflection Sheets

The reflection sheets can be used on a daily or weekly basis. At the end of the day or half-day, a teaching team may sit down for five to ten minutes to discuss how things went. The reflection sheet can then be used to focus the agenda of that brief discussion and serve as a recording tool. Or, before planning for the next week, a teacher can review how this week has gone. He uses the reflection framework to help with the review and to assist in planning follow-up to the events that occurred and the children's responses to the activities.

By combining the planning and reflection processes, teachers are more fully aware of children's needs. There is a connection from week to week, building on children's interests and capabilities. Assessment information gained through observing children is integrated into planning for the next set of activities. The curriculum flows more smoothly.

When either of these forms is used in combination with the planning framework, a teacher has a written history of classroom life. These written records can also provide direction and ideas for the next activities, projects, academic learning, individual adjustments, and challenges. They can provide the basis for family communication or for teaching team conversations. Administrators can review the planning and reflection frameworks and get accurate information for supervision and evaluation.

Mary: *"I've jotted down those things that are not working so that I can use that information to think about in the next week."*

Vicki: *"The reflection part is very helpful, especially more so at the beginning of the year. You can note what worked and what didn't, who had trouble and who didn't. This would really help in working with your teaching assistants."*

Mary: *"Other things I'm looking for in a planning model is a space to write planning and reviewing activities ['plan, do, review'], but I've found they sometimes can go in other places. . . . Maybe a space to focus on transitions might be helpful. This is always the area that is most troublesome."*

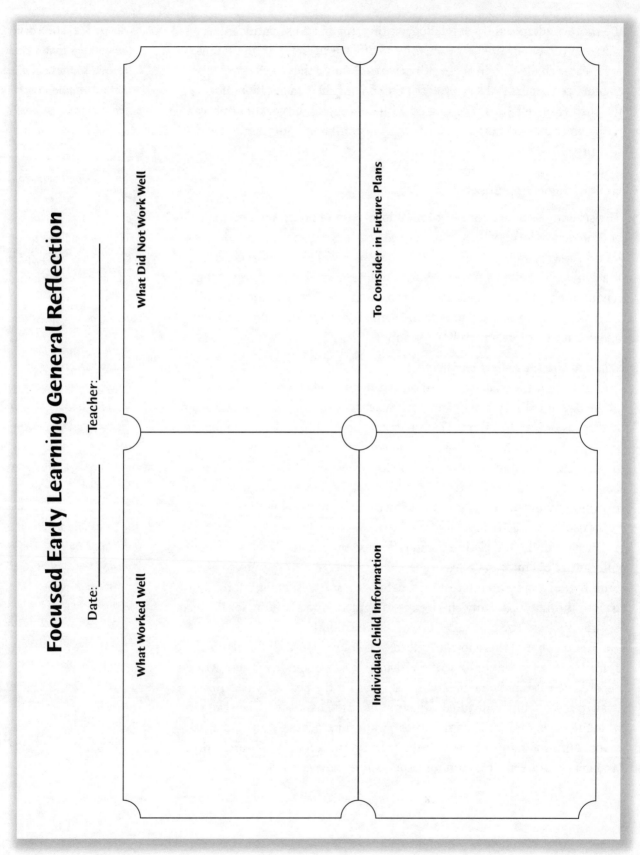

General Reflection Sheet

Creating Your Own Planning and Reflection Frameworks

Preschool teachers are unique individuals—just like the children they teach. Their teaching styles vary. The emphasis they place on their classroom activities reflects their special talents and interests, background, and experience. To recognize that uniqueness, this book also includes the same framework design for both planning and reflection with blank boxes. *(See the appendix.)* Fill in the ways you integrate curricular approaches in your classroom. You may wish to use some from the Focused Early Learning frameworks and add your own. Some teachers have added "classroom rituals;" others have added "music." The Focused Early Learning framework design is by no means all-inclusive. Please take ownership of the framework and make it work for you.

Some programs require teachers to post their weekly plans for parents and family members, as well as supervisors, to review. The Focused Early Learning Frameworks include some information that might be considered confidential, or inappropriate for such posting. The areas on the framework to consider with this in mind include: Steps to Relationship Building, Individual Adjustment, and Focused Observations. Teachers who wish to post their plans may want to make a photocopy of only those areas that do not include personal information about plans for specific children and post that photocopy instead of the whole framework.

Using the Framework in Your Classroom

The following chapters, then, take various sections identified on the frameworks and guide teachers through the process of using them for both planning and reflection. In each chapter, specific areas are highlighted. Sample plans and reflection frameworks from preschool teachers around the country are included for you to review. Each chapter will include a "Focus on Teaching" section, which will help integrate the planning and reflection process with the actual implementation of an integrated preschool curriculum.

This book will include several completed plans. However, these plans are just examples. They are not meant to be used in your classroom. They were created by teachers for their settings, knowing their children and their needs. The only people who can determine the best plans for a classroom are the teachers who work in that setting. They know the strengths

---

All five of the teachers found the frameworks helpful in working with others. Both Vicki and Diana found it allowed more open communication and dialogue with their teaching assistants. Pam used it with a student teacher and reported that her student teacher really had a clear idea of the expectations of a preschool teacher who is planning the classroom. Mary and Valerie each shared the framework with their principals, who both commented on how involved the plans were and how many areas were being addressed.

Valerie: *"In the past I had nothing to give to my supervisor to help her see what I'm doing in the classroom."*

Mary: *"Our principal was telling the kindergarten teachers that they need to do more play in the classroom and one teacher made the comment, 'At least that will make planning easier. I'll just write* Play *across the page.' So, I showed her my plans so she could see how involved they were and how many areas were being addressed. I don't know if that will impact her, but who knows?"*

> **Pam:** *"I like to include information on my plans about the specialists who work in my classroom as well. Sometimes our speech therapist conducts our large group activity, or leads a special language group for a small number of children. I didn't always feel there was enough room under the group activities to include this."*

> **Diana:** *"I copy the parts of the plans that include Child-Led Exploration in the Rich Classroom Environment, the academic pieces, and the large and small group times, and post that for my parents to see. The rest of the plan is for me and my aide to review and refer to as we go about our day and is kept on my desk."*

and weaknesses in the room arrangement. They see the ways children succeed and are challenged on a daily basis. Therefore, be careful that you don't assume that the plans included in this book will be right for your setting. When you use the Focused Early Learning Frameworks, you will fill out your own planning forms based on your knowledge of the materials you have access to, the amount of adult support you have, and the needs of your particular group of children. To truly be an individualized curriculum, all of these factors must be taken into consideration.

Chapter 3 will focus on creating a rich classroom environment. Setting up the learning areas, planning with learning goals in mind, and figuring out exactly when to change materials and activities, will be discussed.

Building relationships with individual children will be explored in depth in chapter 4. We will look at ways to get to know each child and to make individual adjustments in the classroom to best help, support, and challenge each child.

Chapter 5 will help teachers to incorporate academic and developmental learning activities throughout the planning framework, determining how to make "academics" developmentally appropriate for preschoolers.

Chapter 6 will focus on planning for the tremendous physical energy of preschool children by looking at the areas on the form marked Physical Energy Outlets and Outdoors Explorations.

Chapter 7 will focus on balancing child choice with teacher-led activities. We will look again at the classroom environment and how to use it effectively with preschoolers so that chaos does not reign. Teacher-led small and large group times will also be discussed in depth. What are the best ways to organize activities so that children are engaged and successful?

In chapter 8, we'll explore planning for ongoing projects and studies, and being responsive to the emerging interests of the children. Chapter 9 will demonstrate how to integrate all of the above into focused observations and assessing children's learning.

chapter 3

The Focused Early Learning Weekly Planning Framework

Date:_____ Teacher:_____

Child-led Exploration in the Rich Classroom Environment

Art

Sensory Table

Blocks

Library

Writing Center

Dramatic Play

Ongoing Projects

Manipulatives

Scientific Inquiries

Math Moments

Reading and Writing

Individual Adjustments

Steps to Relationship Building

Creating a Rich Classroom Environment

In preschool classrooms, the room arrangement and presentation of materials are essential components of the curriculum. The classroom environment can provide learning opportunities, create a sense of community, and maintain a positive atmosphere where productive interactions occur among children and adults. Children take the lead in exploring the classroom. Teachers provide the structure for that exploration by the way they organize the areas of the classroom, the materials in those areas, and by the way they carefully plan for the use of those materials. Planning and organizing the environment is part of teaching. Interacting with the children within the classroom environment completes the preschool teaching process.

The Focused Early Learning planning framework includes a large, centrally located box identifying seven learning areas that should be available daily to children: blocks, art, sensory table, dramatic play, library, manipulatives, and writing center.

In the classroom, each learning area is distinctively set up as a separate space. Shelving and tables help delineate that space. Baskets, bins, and tubs help to organize a variety of materials. Shelves are labeled with photos, pictures, and/or words. Order is communicated clearly to children by this arrangement. As children follow this clear order when using materials and putting them away by themselves, they develop independence.

Children can return to an area and do the same thing again and again. Or they can combine materials in different ways. The materials are extensive enough that teachers do not have to change anything in the areas daily or even weekly. Instead, there is a range of possibilities for using the basic materials available. Later in this chapter, in the "Focus on Teaching" section, you will find suggestions for organizing the environment and continually evaluating its effectiveness. References to other books and resources about preschool classroom environments are included.

Planning for the Environment

Initially, your goal is for the children to explore all of the learning areas in the classroom. You want them to discover the range of materials available and try using those materials in the ways they were intended. For example, you want them to try putting together the various manipulatives and puzzles you have in your manipulative area, and you want them to construct and build with the blocks in the block area.

Developmental goals that describe what the children will do through that exploration and discovery are written in the planning framework. It is not necessary to list all of the materials involved, nor is such a listing helpful to the planning process. Instead, by writing down your goals for the learning area, you will keep yourself focused on the purposes for activities and the ways you and your teaching colleagues can support learning and development. Each goal can then be directly correlated with expectations for preschool children's performance and tied to assessment information. *(See chapter 9 for more on tying these goals to various assessment tools.)* Here is Darlene's completed plan for her classroom environment focusing on one of the first weeks of the school year.

> **Child-led Exploration in the Rich Classroom Environment**
>
> **Blocks**
> CONSTRUCT & BUILD WITH WOODEN & PLASTIC BLOCKS
>
> **Dramatic Play**
> IMITATE HOUSEHOLD & FAMILY LIFE & TASKS WITH COOKING UTENSILS & DRESS-UP CLOTHES
>
> **Manipulatives**
> USE FINE MOTOR SKILLS TO PICK UP & USE SMALL ITEMS
>
> **Art**
> EXPERIMENT WITH PAINTS, MARKERS, SCISSORS & PASTE
>
> **Ongoing Projects**
> EXPLORE THE CLASSROOM
>
> **Sensory Table**
> POUR, MEASURE, COMPARE AMOUNTS OF WATER WITH MEASUREMENT TOOLS
>
> **Library**
> LOOK AT PICTURES & PRINT IN BOOKS
>
> **Writing Center**
> USE WRITING TOOLS TO MAKE MARKS IN IMITATION OF WRITING

Darlene's Plan Week 1

Notice that the plan for each learning area focuses on exploring and using the materials available in that area. The description tells *what the child will do* with those materials. It also identifies what developmental goals will be met: "construct and build, imitate family life, use fine motor skills, use writing tools, etc." It does not tell *what the teacher will do*. It focuses on the child and gives clear ideas for what teachers can watch for, suggest to the children, facilitate or help the children do. Also, notice that in the box labeled "Ongoing Projects," Darlene has written "Explore the classroom." There is no need to add any other topic of study at this time. Helping the children learn more about the various areas of the classroom and try out the many possibilities in each of those areas is enough to focus on in the first weeks. Later in this chapter, and more in-depth in chapter 8, you will learn ways to determine and incorporate projects and studies in the environment.

When to Change the Goals or Materials

The above goals could continue for several weeks. The selection of materials in each area should be extensive and rich enough so the children will continue to explore the possibilities for using those materials. The role of the teacher is to encourage that exploration, to watch what the children repeat and practice, and to suggest different ways of using the materials. Since there are many possibilities present, the plans for the areas do not need to change every day or every week.

The following circumstances, however, warrant change:

- The children are ignoring a particular area.
- The children are bored with what's available (they may say they are bored; they may appear bored in their interactions; or they may change the area themselves, bringing new materials or doing different things with those materials).

Vicki: *"The book really helped me become more aware of planning for the rich classroom environment with goals in mind for each activity. 'Art' could be following directions, or using a variety of materials to create, or experimenting and exploring, or several different things."*

Pam: *"I really liked planning the learning areas with goals for the children in mind, rather than just listing materials. That made more sense and really made me more accountable to what was happening in those areas."*

> **Valerie:** *"I liked that the framework helped me show that this is what the children will be learning from the block area, the manipulatives, and so on. I'm really doing much better as a teacher because I'm covering the gaps. All the learning goals on what you're doing are on one plan."*
>
> **Diana:** *"I really liked the idea that I don't have to change the areas every week. I'm always telling myself that, but then I go ahead and do it anyway, creating more work for myself. This relieved me of my own internal pressure to keep changing things. And I could see it was better for the kids. They became much more involved and returned to activities again and again."*

- The children's behavior is not productive or positive in an area.
- The materials could be changed to support an interest of the children, a developmental need, or a topic of study or project that has emerged in the classroom.

If none of the above are evident, there is no need to make changes. Once the basic areas are in place, a teacher should be free to interact with the children and observe their explorations. She need not be concerned with constant rearrangement or change. Children appreciate consistency. They relish practicing things over and over again, which is how mastery is attained. If the original materials provided in an area include a range of possibilities, the children should be able to return again and again and become engaged in productive and creative use of those materials. Only when a teacher sees boredom or poor behavior, or wants to follow an interest or a topic of study, should new materials and activities be introduced.

The Reflection Process

It is not necessary to change the plans for all of the areas. It is only necessary to do so for the ones where the above criteria are evident. Using the reflection framework or the general reflection form will help determine what areas of the classroom need changes.

For example, Darlene used her plan #1 (above) for the first week of the fall with her three- to five-year-old students. She watched closely as the children built with blocks, experimented with art materials, used their fine motor skills with manipulatives, and poured and measured water in a variety of containers. Darlene's reflection framework from the first week showed her that no changes were needed in the classroom arrangement.

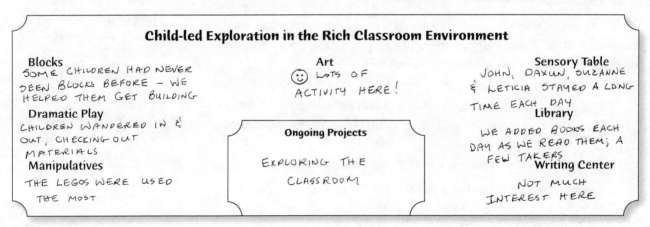

Darlene's Reflection Week 1

However, after the second week, Darlene noticed some differences in the children's engagement with activities and areas in the classroom.

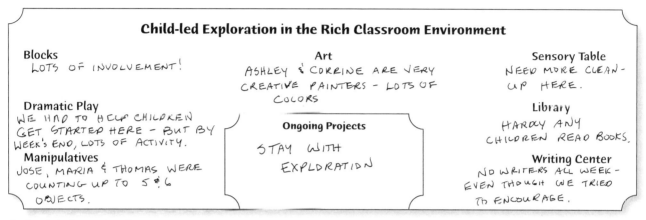

Darlene's Reflection Week 2

As Darlene and her coworkers reflected on the previous week, they noted there was lots of positive engagement in many of the learning areas. However, they saw that the children were not choosing the writing center or library. They decided to change the plans for those two areas alone. In addition, they discussed the need for more adult leadership and interaction in the library and writing center. They included in their plan that, each day, one of them would go to the library to read with the children. They also noted that making the "All About Me" books in the writing center required adult supervision. Through clear communication in their reflection process, they planned for one of the team to be assigned to that area each day. These assignments were written on the planning framework to help everyone involved remember their specific duties for the day or week.

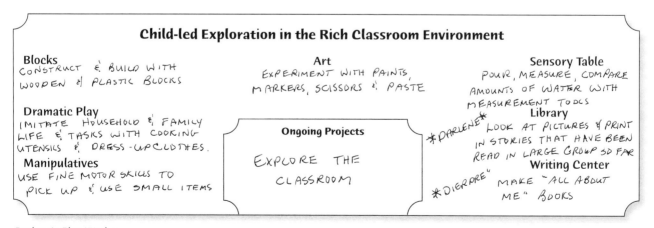

Darlene's Plan Week 3

Changing the Goals for the Learning Areas

Another time to make changes for the classroom environment is when the teacher decides to emphasize different goals using the same materials. In reflection, a teacher may decide that the initial goals from earlier plans really are being met by most of the children. See Genevieve's general reflection form after she implemented similar goals to Darlene's plan #1 for three weeks *(on page 31)*.

Based on her thoughts about the children's accomplishments over those three weeks, Genevieve considered not changing anything in the materials available, or the choices possible. Instead, what she decided to change was the ways children could use those materials and her focus on the children's actions as they tried things out. Genevieve's plan #4 shows the exact same materials with some different goals identified.

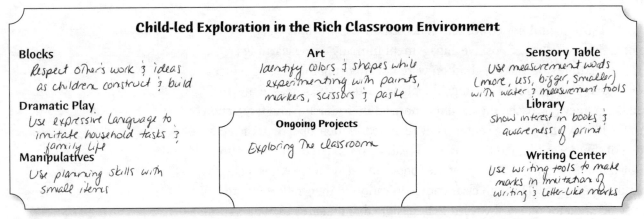

Child-led Exploration in the Rich Classroom Environment

Blocks
Respect other's work & ideas as children construct & build

Dramatic Play
Use expressive language to imitate household tasks & family life

Manipulatives
Use planning skills with small items

Art
Identify colors & shapes while experimenting with paints, markers, scissors & paste

Ongoing Projects
Exploring the classroom

Sensory Table
Use measurement words (more, less, bigger, smaller) with water & measurement tools

Library
Show interest in books & awareness of print

Writing Center
Use writing tools to make marks in imitation of writing & letter-like marks

Genevieve's Plan Week 4

Notice that Genevieve did not have to put out any materials that differ from plan #1. However, she and her colleagues did have different ideas for facilitating the children's use of the materials, or for focusing their interactions and observations of the ways children engage in different activities. The plan changed because the teacher's focus changed. But that new focus did not require new materials or a different room arrangement. It only required a different point of view for the adults in the room.

So many developmental goals can be met by using the basic materials in a preschool classroom in different ways. Some teachers find it helpful to make a list of all of the possible learning goals for each learning area in the environment. When they do so, they often find that each area can help the children develop literacy and math skills, fine motor and language skills, and social/emotional skills. Changing the goals can be a way to make sure that each learning area is being used to its fullest potential by the children.

Focused Early Learning General Reflection

Date: Week #3 9/12/00 Teacher: Genevieve

What Worked Well

The children have started exploring most of the learning areas & using them successfully, meeting our goals. They're still engaged most of the time.

What Did Not Work Well

- Clean-up time chaotic still
- Help children put away paints, etc.
- Circle time needed to be shorter, especially for Jones. — too much adult talk

Individual Child Information

- Jared needs more 1-1 with an adult
- Mariah is so quiet
- Noah & Taylor seem to be pairing up as friends

To Consider in Future Plans

- Anna — Be primary caregiver to Jared
- How can we bring out Mariah?
- Change goals for activities but not materials at this point

Changing the Materials in All Areas of the Environment

Once in a while it may seem that everyone in the classroom could use a dose of new possibilities. Maybe several areas appear to be boring to the children. Or, perhaps lots of behavior problems are arising throughout the classroom. It may then be time to change all of the areas in the environment. Six weeks into the preschool year, Luis sat down with his teaching assistants, Sandra and Suzie, to reflect on the previous week in their classroom and to plan for the next one. In their discussion, they all agreed that the children needed some new activities and materials. They were seeing more wandering behavior and less purposeful exploration. Luis wrote their comments on the reflection framework for week 6.

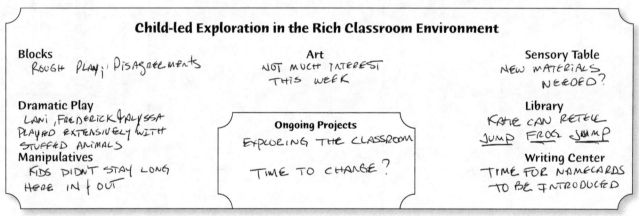

Luis' Reflection Week 6

They all determined that sweeping changes were needed throughout the classroom. Luis was not convinced that it was time to introduce a project or study. However, he and his colleagues decided to add some new materials to various areas. In other areas, they merely changed the ways they would suggest the children use the existing materials. Still their plan reflects the developmental goals they have in mind as the children try out these new plans. Notice that Luis is responding to the children's expressed interest in dramatic play with the stuffed animals. Maybe the veterinarian's office will develop into a full-fledged topic of study after the implementation of the plan for week 7.

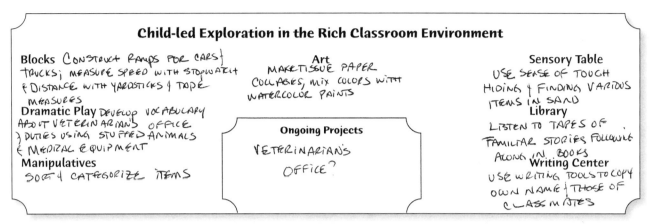

Luis' Plan Week 7

A strong word of caution is needed at this point: Do not feel it is necessary to change all areas of the classroom on a regular basis! Children relish repetition, familiarity, and consistency. They can go more in-depth with activities, develop and refine skills, and complicate their own interactions with materials if they have the opportunity to visit areas again and again. Many teachers create far more work for themselves by assuming they must change their environment daily or weekly. Instead, pay close attention to the children, and only change those areas that need changing. A plan like Luis' will only be necessary once in awhile. It will be more common to use plans like Darlene's or Genevieve's.

Changing Plans to Correlate to an Interest of the Children, a Topic of Study, or a Project

We will explore the whole process of developing emergent curriculum based on interests of the children and taking those interests into an in-depth topic of study or project in chapter 8. However, it is appropriate to note here that when a teacher does decide to focus curriculum around a topic, he may want to change some things in the classroom environment.

So far, all of our plans have shown teachers early in the school year, keeping the focus on exploring the classroom. Mrs. Chang also started this way. However, a bird began building a nest right outside the classroom window. The children started paying attention to the bird and watched her carefully prepare her nest. Mrs. Chang and her teaching assistant noted the children's interest in their weekly reflection discussion and on their general reflection form *(see the next page).*

Focused Early Learning General Reflection

Date: 10/02/00   Teacher: Mrs. Chang

What Worked Well

Good response to movement activities by most children

Great interest in bird building nest outside of classroom

Name recognition improving

What Did Not Work Well

Cooking activity took too long — too much adult involvement rather than kids

Some throwing sand at sand table again

Need more copies of favorite books — some fighting in class library

Individual Child Information

Sean still has difficulty following routines — especially transitioning.

Josie Did Not Want To dance — let her watch until she's ready

Could Susie help her? Be her friend?

To Consider in Future Plans

Add Bird activities to classroom

Supervise sand more carefully? Or change materials?

Mrs. Chang's Reflection

They decided to follow up on the children's interests and provide some bird-related activities throughout the classroom. In the following plan for the classroom environment, notice that some areas now focus on to the topic of birds, while others do not.

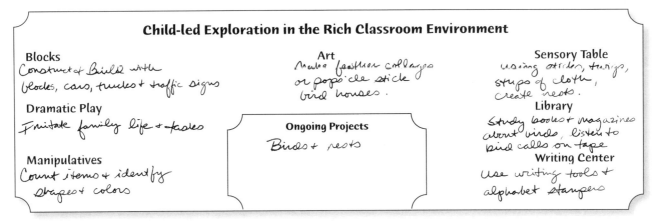

Child-led Exploration in the Rich Classroom Environment

Blocks
Construct + Build with blocks, cars, trucks + traffic signs

Dramatic Play
Imitate family life + tasks

Manipulatives
Count items + identify shapes + colors

Art
Make feather collages or popsicle stick bird houses.

Ongoing Projects
Birds + nests

Sensory Table
using sticks, twigs, strips of cloth, create nests.

Library
Study books + magazines about birds, listen to bird calls on tape

Writing Center
Use writing tools + alphabet stampers

Mrs. Chang's Plan

Mrs. Chang changed only the areas of the environment that made sense to correlate to birds and nests. Many teachers rack their brains trying to figure out correlation to topics for every area of the classroom. Many topics do not fit with every one of the learning areas in the classroom. Some teachers then feel compelled to make new materials (such as bird matching games) to fit everything around a topic. This is not necessary!

When learning more about birds, changing the materials in the block area does not make sense. However, changing art, library, and sensory table materials does. The basic classroom environment does not need the extra layer of a topic in every area. Instead, think carefully about which areas lend themselves to helping the children explore a topic or engage in a project, and only make changes in those areas.

Of course, Mrs. Chang planned for other bird activities to happen in the classroom too, such as stories, songs, bird-watching, walks outdoors, and so on. More of her plans are included in chapter 8.

Focus on Teaching

So many adults outside the early childhood education field think that teaching is equivalent only to *instruction*. They see teaching as telling children what to do or imparting knowledge and concepts through lectures and discussions. Preschool educators know that teaching includes much more—and setting up the environment in a way that is conducive to independent learning through exploration is indeed teaching.

For example, preschool teachers know that the room arrangement and presentation of materials can deeply affect children's behavior. Consider traffic flow and noise levels. If the children's work is constantly interrupted when other children pass by, they will become frustrated and may strike out at others. However, if traffic flow is directed by organizing the classroom in such a way that shelves and tables block any running paths and protect areas for block building, or dramatic play, the children will feel their work is important and protected. The arrangement of furniture and shelves directs children toward the productive use of materials in specific areas. Noise levels are considered so that materials that tend toward greater physical and verbal involvement are placed near each other. Materials that tend toward quieter use are also grouped together.

Consider the classroom arrangement on the facing page. Do you see the organization strategies in use here?

Every teacher's classroom space is different in the square footage, the arrangement of windows and doors, the availability of electrical outlets, and the accessibility to sinks and restrooms. No classroom arrangement in a book will match your own. However, basic room organization that helps preschool children function as independently as possible can be done. There are some wonderful resources to consider for guidance in organizing the environment. Here's a short list:

The Creative Curriculum®, by Diane Trister Dodge and Laura J. Colker
Creating Inclusive Classrooms, by Ellen R. Daniels and Kay Stafford
Reflecting Children's Lives: A Handbook for Planning Child-Centered Curriculum, by Deb Curtis and Margie Carter
The Inclusive Early Childhood Classroom: Easy Ways to Adapt Learning Centers for All Children, by Patti Gould and Joyce Sullivan
Big As Life, by Stacey York
Designs for Living and Learning, by Margie Carter and Deb Curtis
Classroom Routines that Really Work for Pre-K and Kindergarten, by Kathleen Hayes and Rennee Creange

Each of these books includes extensive lists of materials to put into learning areas and ways to organize the classroom itself.

Many teachers who use these resources to help them set up the classroom environment report that behavior problems dramatically lessen. The children's use of materials becomes more productive. They stay with activities longer. They participate more willingly in cleanup. Teachers are no longer running interference or playing "referee" as frequently as before. Chaos does not reign. Instead, the classroom has a busy hum of activity.

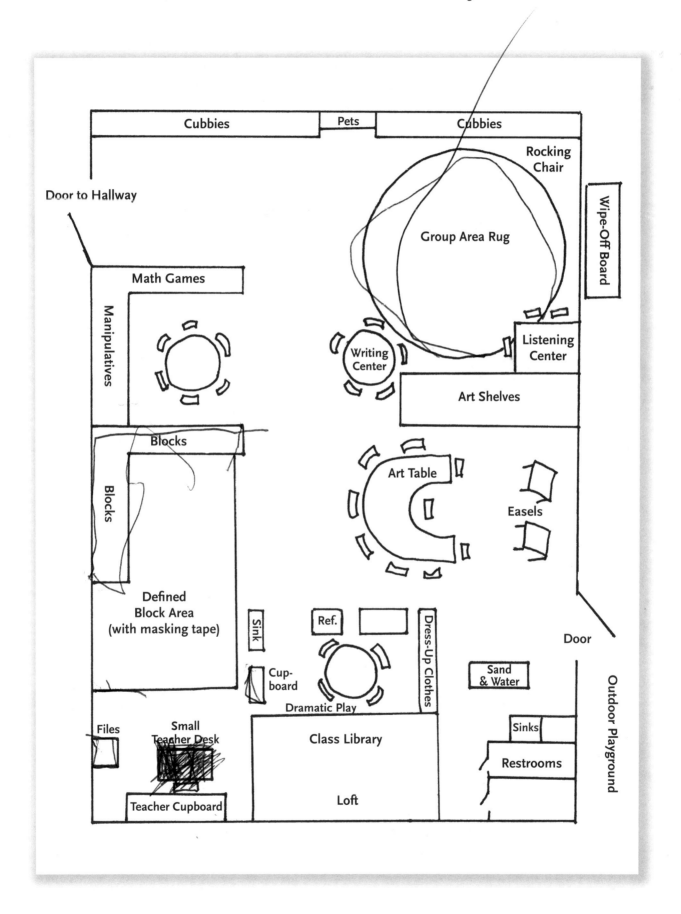

Teachers find more opportunities to interact with the children and observe them at work. Many teachers say they can relax and enjoy their time with the children much more fully.

Continually Evaluating the Environment

A teacher carefully plans the basic environment. She recognizes the importance of communicating order, structure, and extensive possibilities for the productive use of materials. She also continually evaluates the classroom environment to see how it is working. How effectively is the setup contributing to the children's comfort, risk taking, and learning?

In *Dimensions of Teaching-Learning Environments* (1984), Betty Jones and Liz Prescott offer a different perspective that can be helpful in evaluating room arrangement and organization of materials in a classroom. They identify five dimensions to consider:

1. Softness/Hardness
2. Open/Closed
3. Simple/Complex
4. Intrusion/Seclusion*
5. High Mobility/Low Mobility

Through interaction with others (intrusion), to what extent does a child get novelty, stimulation, and enrichment? To what extent does the physical setting permit the children to be alone? To be in small groups?

The authors encourage teachers to view the classroom environment with the idea that children need a full continuum of possibilities within each of these dimensions. Here are some of the suggestions that Jones and Prescott give for each of the dimensions. Can you think of others? If you were to walk around your classroom with a critical eye, what would you see evident in each of these dimensions? What's missing?

One way to evaluate the effectiveness of a classroom environment is to get down on your knees and look at the room from a child's perspective. As adults, our height puts us at a disadvantage in seeing exactly how obstacles and traffic patterns are laid out from a preschooler's perspective.

In *Reflecting Children's Lives: A Handbook for Planning Child-Centered Curriculum* (1996), Deb Curtis and Margie Carter have identified the following characteristics, which help to create an environment where both teachers and children love to spend time:

- Materials are visible, accessible, aesthetically organized, and attractive to children.

Softness/Hardness Dimension

Soft or Sensory Responsive → ← **Hard or Less Sensory Responsive**

- Cozy furniture
- Large carpet or rug
- Grass
- Sand/dirt
- Furry animals
- Sling swings
- Playdough
- Very messy materials—fingerpaint, clay, mud, water added to sand
- Water
- People's laps

- Rounded wooden shelves
- Manipulatives with a variety of textures
- Floors
- Tables
- Wooden or plastic chairs

Open/Closed Dimension

Open | **Relatively Open** | **Closed**

- Dough
- Collage
- Sand
- Water play
- Open shelves and/or cupboards
- Materials are visible and reachable

- Unit blocks
- Tinkertoys
- Cuisenaire rods
- Manipulatives
- Behind unlocked doors
- Materials are visible but not reachable

- Puzzles
- Matching games
- Worksheets
- Locked cupboards
- High shelves

Simple/Complex Dimension

Simple → ← **Complex**

- Materials have one obvious use such as a tricycle, a slide, a workbook page

- Two different play materials to manipulate or improvise with such as sand table with tools, play house with supplies or cooking utensils
- Materials that have more than one correct use, such as sensory and art materials
- Other opportunities for improvisation, creativity, and unpredictability such as art, woodworking, books, animals

Intrusion/Seclusion Dimension

Open Areas | **Partially Screened** | **Insulated** | **Secluded**

- No boundaries exist
- Activity tables or easels set against walls or with one or two-sided protection
- Areas that accommodate only small groups of children
- Close, cozy spaces for one or two children only

High Mobility/Low Mobility Dimension

High Mobility → ← **Low Mobility**

- Large muscle activities
- Active movement from place to place

- Small muscle activities
- Sedentary activity

- Diverse textures, shapes, and elements of the natural world are present.
- The space is flexible.
- There is an ample supply of "loose parts": open-ended materials such as large pieces of fabric, corks, tubes, and plastic rings.
- Children's lives and interests are represented throughout the room.
- Visual images represent a range of roles and cultural expressions.

Using Jones's and Prescott's five dimensions—looking at things from a child's perspective—or considering Curtis' and Carter's suggestions can help us continually evaluate the effectiveness of our classroom environment.

One Teacher's Story

Carole kept a pad of sticky notes and a pen in her pocket. As she interacted with the children throughout her preschool classroom, she paid attention to times when she noted boredom or poor behavior. She placed a sticky note somewhere in that area of the classroom, out of reach of the children. At the end of the week, she and her teaching assistant, Armando, noted where the sticky notes were located and took time to carefully examine that particular area of the classroom. They asked themselves important questions such as:

- Are new materials needed here?
- Is the furniture arranged in ways that are conducive to traffic flow and personal space?
- Is more adult presence necessary?
- Should the number of children in that area be limited or extended?

They made changes as they answered those questions, then observed closely to see the resulting behaviors and engagement with the materials in those areas.

For example, one week, Carole and Armando noted lots of yelling and fighting among the children in the block area. Lots of sticky notes ended up on the wall above the block area. The next week, they both watched carefully and realized that a traffic path went right through the rug area where many of the block constructions were being built. As the children walked by on their way to other classroom areas, they inadvertently knocked against the constructions, causing them to fall, much to the dismay of the builders. Carole and Armando rearranged the shelving in the block area to eliminate this traffic path and rerouted it around the shelves to protect the block constructions.

chapter 4

The Focused Early Learning Weekly Planning Framework

Date: _____ Teacher: _____

Child-led Exploration in the Rich Classroom Environment

- Blocks
- Dramatic Play
- Manipulatives
- Reading and Writing
- Art
- Ongoing Projects
- Math Moments
- Sensory Table
- Library
- Writing Center
- Scientific Inquiries

Steps to Relationship Building

Individual Adjustments

Developing Relationships with Children and Families

Erik Erikson, the developmental theorist, identified progressive stages in child development. Up to age three, he said, the child's primary task is to develop trust in others, and autonomy for himself. The three- to five-year-old's task is to engage in initiative: trying things out, creating, representing experience. The six- to eight-year-old's task is to engage in industry: using ever-growing skills toward an end, developing competence.

The development of trust precedes autonomy. It precedes initiative. It precedes industry. So, even for preschool children who are in the stage of initiative, trust must be developed in every new setting and relationship. For this reason, as part of a good preschool curriculum, teachers work hard to assure children of their best intentions for them. They make sure the classroom is warm and inviting and includes cubbies or areas for each child's things to be stored, places for the children's artwork to be displayed, and ways to invite the families to be a part of the program.

Relationship Building and the Focused Early Learning Frameworks

As teachers get to know each child, they can use the Focused Early Learning frameworks to help them plan steps to relationship building with each child. This task is not left to chance. Instead, it is included on the weekly planning and reflection sheets. Teachers emphasize its importance by thinking about relationships with the children in advance, by implementing steps to strengthen those relationships, and by reflecting on what happens with the children each week in the classroom. And all is written down.

On the planning framework there is a box labeled "Steps to Relationship Building." Here, a teacher writes down specific actions he plans to take in relationship building with individual children. Another box, labeled "Individual Adjustments," also involves this attention to individual children. Here, a teacher writes what changes to existing activities will be made to help specific children be successful. This attention to individual children helps strengthen their sense of trust. They recognize that their teachers care deeply about them.

Steps to Relationship Building

Building strong relationships with children is an essential task that involves many possibilities. Assuring a child that he can trust his teacher takes up much of the first days in a classroom for young children. Teachers do this by warmly welcoming each child. They carefully learn each child's name and use it frequently. They pay close attention to initial signals the child sends out about her personality, her approach to learning, her social comfort levels, and her relationship with her family members. When a teacher senses that a child withdraws any time she is touched, that teacher is careful not to touch the child unnecessarily. When a teacher sees a child inappropriately approaching other children to play, she makes an effort to provide assistance and modeling for that child, stepping in at just the right time, and giving the words for the child to say: "Can I play too?"

Getting to know a child's family is a way of building a relationship with both the child and the family. Having an open-door policy in the classroom for the families communicates to them that they can trust this place for their child. Becoming familiar with a child's cultural background can help to build the relationship. If the child's family speaks a language other than English, communicating in the home language can help immensely in building a positive relationship. Even using a few words, or providing books or posters in the child's language or showing cultural aspects familiar to that child can be helpful.

On the planning framework, a teacher may write some general steps he is going to take to build relationships with all of the children. This is more often the case at the beginning of the school year.

Here are some examples of more general teachers' plans for steps to relationship building with the children in their classrooms.

Steps to Relationship Building

Show children where their cubby and personal art gallery are located. Give them name card and help them sign in each day.

Gayle's Plan

Steps to Relationship Building

Help children learn routines and daily schedules with lots of reminders and consistent pattern of activities.

Vee's Plan

Steps to Relationship Building

INVITE FAMILIES TO SEND IN 4-5 FAMILY PHOTOS. MAKE A "CLASS FAMILY PHOTO ALBUM" TO BE PLACED IN OUR CLASSROOM LIBRARY.

Darlene's Plan

Steps to Relationship Building

Review respecting others' feelings and property at large group time and throughout the day.

Valerie's Plan

As teachers get to know individual children's personalities and approaches to learning, the plans written in the "Steps to Relationship Building" section will name specific children and will focus on helping them be more successful at specific times of the day. Then, in reflection, teachers can note exactly what occurred with that child during the week and make plans to support that child.

Here are some examples of teachers' plans and reflections for specific children in their classroom.

Steps to Relationship Building

Katelin, Colton and Cameron wandered during activity time - not sure what to do? Need adult help? Group with other children?

Pam's Reflection

Steps to Relationship Building

Donna will help Katelin join a group of others. Pam will focus on Colton and Cameron and do the same.

Pam's Plan

Steps to Relationship Building

Anastasia does not like to be touched by teachers or other children - but will initiate a hug herself.

Vicki's Reflection

Steps to Relationship Building

Be careful not to touch Anastasia - let her initiate. Help other children to do the same.

Vicki's Plan

Steps to Relationship Building

Several new children will be joining our class in the next few weeks. How can we make them feel welcomed?

Linde's Reflection

Steps to Relationship Building

Pair the new children with children who have been here since Sept. for social support.

Linde's Plan

Focus on Teaching

The following list identifies some possibilities for steps to relationship building that might be included in a teacher's planning framework. By no means is this list complete. Teachers do so many things to build relationships with children and families. Can you think of more ideas? The possibilities are endless, aren't they?

Possibilities for Steps to Relationship Building

- Welcome a child by name with a warm smile.
- Touch a child (rub a back or arm, give a hug).
- Look a child in the eye (wink, smile, laugh).
- Welcome family members to the classroom.
- Greet and chat with family members at pick-up and drop-off times.
- Sit with a child (seek out a child at circle time or activity time).
- Invite a child to sit on your lap.
- Use a child's home language or provide materials in that language.
- Respect a child's personality (avoid pushing a quiet child to speak; avoid touching a child who is sensitive to touch).
- Ask to play or work alongside a child (imitate his interactions with materials).
- Let a child take the lead (go first, answer a question, give an idea).
- Ask a child to be a special helper.
- Give a child positive feedback ("Wow! Look at all the colors you used!" "You jumped really high!").
- Set limits with a child ("No, I will not let you hurt yourself. That jumping platform is too high. Let's make it a little smaller, and put a mat underneath.").
- Allow a child to have some quiet, private time.
- Recognize that a child has lots of physical energy to spend ("Let's get out the hoops and build a hopping path.").

Any of the above steps could be written on the planning framework in the "Steps to Relationship Building" box. Specify the children's names, or write general steps for the class as a whole. Many other possibilities will arise as you get to know the children in your program better. Do not feel limited to the list above. Be open to all of the possibilities to relate with the children in your care.

Individual Adjustments

Making adjustments in the classroom with a specific child in mind is another way to build relationships with the children. In the box labeled "Individual Adjustments," a teacher writes what changes to existing activities will be made to help specific children be successful. This is truly individualizing the curriculum. A rich classroom environment can only provide opportunities for individual children. A teacher's careful planning of how to support the child in those opportunities, or to change the possibilities, is where individualization occurs. No longer are you thinking of

Vicki: *"It's so interesting to me that you have to approach each child differently. For example, we have a girl who, if you touch her, will yell at you, "Don't touch me!" Yet, she will come and sit on your lap. We have learned to let her initiate physical contact. Some children, you know right away when you greet them at the door how they're doing. That's because you're very attuned to that relationship."*

Valerie: *"My school district has adopted a self-esteem and character building curriculum for K through 12. I took the activities and adapted them for my preschoolers. I write the plans for these activities in the 'Steps to Relationship Building' section of the framework. Sometimes we talk about feelings or good and bad actions. It's really fit well here in the plan."*

> **Pam:** *"I used the 'Steps to Relationship Building' section to help children form a group to play a game. It helped me think about the quiet children who are often by themselves, and strategize ways to bring them into relationships with other children and adults."*

activities for all the children. Now, within those activities, you're thinking about each individual child.

As you get to know a child, you will ask yourself questions about her success in the classroom. Are there materials that she chooses more often than others? Why? Are those materials appropriate at her level of capability? Are they at the level where she is practicing and almost mastering them? Does she avoid materials? Why? Do those materials require the use of skills she hasn't yet acquired?

Providing materials that match a child's capabilities can be a way to build the relationship. Noticing that a child is frustrated with fifteen-piece puzzles, a teacher may get out puzzles with eight to ten pieces. Seeing that a child is bored with simple alphabet matching games, a teacher may encourage a child to match cards with classmates' names instead. Pay close attention to the child's level of developmental accomplishments and make adjustments in the curriculum to not only match that level, but also to challenge the child to move ahead in skills, knowledge, and concepts.

Some weeks, the individual adjustments you plan are a result of observations of children from the previous week. So, often, the reflection process will help guide planning for individual adjustments. Then, in reflection the following week, evaluate how successful those adjustments were. Getting to know each child well, and helping and supporting him to be successful in a preschool classroom is an ongoing process that can be documented clearly in both the planning and reflection frameworks. The documentation can then be used as assessment information in observations and portfolios. We'll discuss more fully the observation and assessment process in chapter 9.

On the following pages are some examples of teachers' plans for the "Individual Adjustments" section of the frameworks. A reflection form from a previous week, a plan for an individual adjustment for the child, and a reflection form with the results of the adjustment are included so the full cycle of planning and reflection can clearly be seen.

Individual Adjustments

Grecia and Ricardo constantly push at each other, talk loudly, argue sometimes at group time or snack when seated next to each other.

Stephanie is so easily frightened — ask Mom about her fears at home.

Linde's Reflection Week 1

Individual Adjustments

Seating at groups + snack — do not put Grecia + Ricardo together; either separate tables or with an adult between.

Provide emotional support to Stephanie for her fear of animals, wind and loud noises.

Linde's Plan Week 2

Individual Adjustments

Circle time was smoother with Grecia and Ricardo separated. Grecia is making friends with Vanessa. Who can we encourage as a friend for Ricardo?

Stephanie likes carrying the Mr. Turtle puppet for comfort.

Linde's Reflection Week 2

Individual Adjustments

Austin & David have delayed language responses - yet seem to understand most questions and comments directed towards them. If you stay with them, they will eventually respond.

Valerie's Reflection Week 1

Individual Adjustments

Both Valerie & Marie will allow extra time for Austin & David to respond, and will set up opportunities for them to point or touch and speak whenever possible.

Valerie's Plan Week 2

Individual Adjustments

Austin & David did better with the physical aspect of pointing & touching. We'll talk over with our speech therapist to help language responses. Should we consider a communication board?

Valerie's Reflection Week 2

Individual Adjustments

Rebecca, Jason and Heather are all completing the alphabet puzzle easily. Time for the matching game with upper & lower case?

Jaret makes guns with unifix cubes daily — Can we get him to do something else?

Linde's Reflection Week 1

Individual Adjustments

Put out alphabet matching game at manipulatives — Issue as a challenge to all children, but especially Rebecca, Jason & Heather.

Give Jaret a "special assignment" to measure the classroom, doorways, tables, etc. with unifix cubes.

Linde's Plan Week 2

Individual Adjustments

Heather & Jason successfully matched many alphabet letters; Rebecca lost interest. Destiny & Kaleigh made up their own game finding the letters in their names.

Jaret "measured" everything in sight! We had him report to the class. He did so with a big smile.

Linde's Reflection Week 2

> **Mary:** *"I appreciate the inclusion of the 'Steps to Relationship Building' and 'Individual Adjustments' sections because they are ways to focus on those issues as they come up and demonstrate that these are being addressed. It's a record of the week in this way. I've been writing down things as they happen, too, to record work done in relationships."*

> **Vicki:** *"The individual adjustments really tied the lesson plans to our IEP [Individual Education Plan] goals for each child. There are a couple of kids who cannot handle sitting with the large group for story. So, we could plan separate activities for that child with my assistant. We would write something like this on the framework: 'CJ will read one-on-one with Joyce and point to the pictures,' which would tie back to CJ's IEP goals as well. It helped us get much more specific in thinking about the kids."*

Focus on Teaching

Getting to know a child's personality and dispositions to learning can also determine individual adjustments. Several of the suggestions in the list of steps for relationship building could be used as individual adjustments as well. For example, if you learn that a child is routinely a leader in the classroom, you might want to offer a number of leadership opportunities. You also may want to help this child learn to work cooperatively with other children and may set up some situations where she is the follower rather than the leader. For a child who does not take the lead very often, you may want to set up nonthreatening opportunities for him to shine in front of the group once in a while.

A child with great curiosity needs opportunities to investigate. A child who does not try new things naturally may need new activities brought to her. All of these individual adjustments can be written on the planning framework. The following list again is not all-inclusive, but gives some possibilities. What else would you add?

Individual Adjustments

- Offer materials that are more successful for the child.
- Offer materials that are more challenging for the child.
- Help the child ask another child to play or to use their words to express their feelings.
- Help the child join another group already engaged in play or work.
- Provide language modeling for a child ("Can I play with you?" "No, I don't like that").
- Offer opportunities for leadership.
- Pair up specific children to support and help each other.
- Bring new materials or activities to a more reticent, or set-in-his-ways, child.
- Challenge an inquisitive child to investigate something more fully.
- Recognize a child's sensorimotor responses (for example, avoid forcing a reluctant child to fingerpaint with her hands; rather, accommodate by giving her sticks to paint with, while allowing a child who loves the feel of paint to paint away).
- Prevent behavior problems by anticipating trouble (avoid letting two specific children sit together; sit with a child at circle time, rub his back, or provide a lap for comfort and self-control).
- Help a child cope with difficult situations (comfort a frightened child in a thunderstorm or during a fire drill; talk about sadness at the death of the classroom pet).

As you get to know your children, you will come up with so many different adjustments to be made for each one. This is really at the core of developmentally appropriate curriculum. When teachers take planned steps to build relationships with children and their families, they use the knowledge gained about the children to individualize the curriculum. Each child feels safe and trusts the adults around them. With that sense of safety firmly in place, the children can take advantage of the classroom environment with all of its inviting possibilities. They will explore those possibilities, and take risks, knowing that their teachers are watching carefully and making adjustments to help them be successful.

Again, keep in mind that if you are required to publicly post your weekly plans, you may not want to post the portions of the framework that include personalized information about steps to relationship building and individual adjustments. These are important parts of your everyday planning and help you to individualize your curriculum, but are not appropriate to share with anyone except you and your teaching team, and each child's parents or family members.

How Often Do You Plan for Each Child?

The frequency of writing a plan for each child in the classroom will vary from teacher to teacher. Be careful that your individual adjustments do not get limited only to the children who are more behaviorally challenging. Individual adjustments also include offering challenges to children who are extremely successful in certain skills or activities so they can go further with those skills, or explore other possibilities in using favorite materials.

You may want to set up a time period (the first half of the year or the first two months) for yourself in which you attempt to rotate through every name on your class list in your "Individual Adjustments" box. Each week, you can write about four or five children. Some of us need this kind of task orientation to make sure no child is missed. Or, you may just keep a checklist of the children's names handy and, in the reflection process, check off each time you noted a specific step to relationship building or individual adjustment for each child. Over time, you will see patterns develop and become more aware of the children who are receiving more attention and the children who are being overlooked. Then, you can plan accordingly, focusing on other preschoolers in future weeks.

The "Focused Observations" section of the frameworks (which we'll discuss in chapter 9) is another place where individual attention will be paid

Pam: *"I used the individual adjustments mostly with my kids with IEP goals or my more challenging kids. I would note changes in the environment or particular activities to do with a child, such as 'Sit next to Cameron at circle time.' In fact, I attached my own sheet to the frameworks for individual adjustments for my children with special needs. I just couldn't fit all of the information in the box."* (See Pam's sheet in the appendix.)

Valerie: *"I focused on children's IEP goals on the individual adjustments, and then used my aide's and my reflection discussion to obtain information for my progress reports."*

to the children. Coordinating this assessment piece with the steps to relationship building and the individual adjustments will help insure that each child's development is being analyzed and supported.

Focusing on Families

Preschool children do not arrive at the classroom door in isolation. They come surrounded by the love and concern of their families. Even families with multiple problems love their children. Like their children, parents and other family members need to learn to trust their children's teachers and the program.

Building trust with families, then, is another part of relationship building with children. The frameworks do not include a special box addressing this family connection. However, that does not negate or ignore its importance. Take time to consider all of the program policies that focus on the families of the children in your care. Hopefully, many of the following are routine parts of your program.

Family-Friendly Policies

- *Keep an open door.* Family members can drop in any time to see what's going on in the classroom.
- *Provide regular written communication.* Newsletters, bulletin boards, displays of the children's work, and documentation boards tell the parents about all of the goings-on at preschool.
- *Create opportunities for regular verbal communication.* The teachers are available regularly to converse with the families—greet them, give brief information about how the child is doing, or arrange for more lengthy conversations by telephone or in person when needed.
- *Schedule official family/teacher conferences.* At least once a year (preferably twice) a formal family/teacher conference is scheduled to review the child's progress and development in the classroom, share a portfolio or work collection, and identify goals for the child's continued success.
- *Provide many opportunities for family participation.* Volunteer opportunities in the classroom are available, as well as participation in special family events such as field trips, dinners, open houses, and so forth. There are diverse ways to be involved, so families with many different skills and kinds of availability all have a way to participate.
- *Create and communicate clear policies about solving problems.* Family members are clearly informed of how to raise issues of concern; the teachers and administrative staff are ready to listen respectfully

to problems brought to them by the parents and to work toward a mutually satisfying solution; and the teachers and administrative staff show respect, cultural sensitivity, and a "win-win" attitude when working toward a solution when raising concerns with families.

Building a strong relationship with families strengthens the program itself. Families can be the biggest allies and best advertisers. They can also contribute to the success of the child. If a family is nervous about leaving the child in the classroom, often the child will be nervous as well. If a family is having difficulty communicating with their child's teacher, often the child senses this and may act out in his relationship with the teacher. Making sure that clear communication is ongoing, with a truly welcoming and respectful attitude, will pay off in the long run for the children and for the preschool program. As Valerie said, "I tell my families that I'm there for them. I know their child's disability is hard for them and I want to do everything I can to help them find out what's best for their child." Preschool teachers and family members are on the same team: they are both on the *child's* team.

chapter 5

The Focused Early Learning Weekly Planning Framework

Date:_____ Teacher:_____

Child-led Exploration in the Rich Classroom Environment

- Blocks
- Dramatic Play
- Manipulatives
- Art
- Ongoing Projects
- Math Moments
- Sensory Table
- Library
- Writing Center
- Scientific Inquiries

Reading and Writing

Steps to Relationship Building

Individual Adjustments

Academic and Developmental Learning Activities

Learning is at the core of a good preschool curriculum. In high-quality preschool programs, the teachers set goals to support the healthy development of each child. Those goals include what traditionally might be seen as "academic" goals—learning about books and reading; developing writing skills; learning to count, match, and sort; and exploring various aspects of nature and scientific phenomena.

These academic goals are imbedded in everyday activities in the classroom. Science exploration occurs at the sensory table regularly. Reading and books are part of almost every large group time as well as available in the class library daily. Math activities are provided through manipulatives and block exploration, but also occur in classroom routines like taking attendance or setting the table for snack.

The Focused Early Learning planning framework provides a way for teachers who use an imbedded approach to record the academics that they are planning in all of their activities. In this way, family members, supervisors, and community members can clearly see that "imbedding" does not mean "hoping academics will occur." Instead, the teacher is clear on the academic goals of various activities and notes them on the weekly plan.

On the first page of the framework are three boxes, each highlighting a specific academic content area: reading and writing, math moments, and scientific inquiries. In these boxes teachers write specific activities that will focus on these content areas. The specific activities may be part of daily routines that incorporate reading, math, and science. The activities may take place as part of teacher-led large or small group times. Or they may occur during work or activity time (when the children are exploring the classroom environment).

Here are some examples of plans that show how teachers identified academic goals and planned activities on the planning framework, using the "Reading and Writing," "Math Moments," and "Scientific Inquiries" boxes.

Reading and Writing

Making name cards for sign-in; cubbies & helper chart, introducing class-song book

Gayle's Reading and Writing Plan

Math Moments

Counting children present & absent; setting table for snack with one-to-one correspondence

Gayle's Math Plan

Reading and Writing

Using alphabet stampers at writing center to develop alphabet awareness

Mark's Reading and Writing Plan

Math Moments

Measuring amounts for preparing fruit smoothies; follow sequential steps, 1st, 2nd, 3rd

Mark's Math Plan

Reading and Writing

In class library, give children opportunities to retell familiar stories from the pictures

Genevieve's Reading and Writing Plan

Math Moments

Matching and identifying shapes and numbers by playing bingo games.

Genevieve's Math Plan

Scientific Inquiries

weather observations at circle time; observing water at sensory table

Gayle's Scientific Inquiries Plan

Scientific Inquiries

Investigating balance & gravity in the block area

Genevieve's Scientific Inquiries Plan

Scientific Inquiries

Experiment with "Musical Glasses"

Valerie's Scientific Inquiries Plan

Academics and the Reflection Process

Choosing exactly what learning goals to consider and what specific academic activities to plan will be determined during the reflection process. As you reflect back on the week and what you saw in the classroom, you will ask yourself questions like the following to help you focus on the children's academic skills. What do the children already know and do related to reading, writing, math, and science? What is the level at which they can demonstrate a concept or a skill with some adult help, but haven't quite mastered it yet? (Vygotsky called this the "zone of proximal development.") Then record these observations on the reflection sheet.

When you are ready to use the planning framework for the next week, those observations will guide you in choosing materials and activities to extend the children's academic learning. For example, if the children are routinely counting to five with one-to-one correspondence, it may be time to introduce activities counting to ten. If children are capable of writing their first names, it may be time to introduce name cards with their last names on them as well.

Just as was demonstrated with individual adjustments, teachers will include the academic areas in their reflections and then plan academic learning activities according to the children's successes and challenges in the classroom.

Mary: *"I like including reading and writing, math moments, and scientific inquiries. There are many times during the day where these are addressed but they are not reflected in plans. For instance, many things we do during circle time or outdoor time address these academic areas."*

Pam: *"Including these areas on the framework really made me think 'what are we learning related to reading, writing, math, and science?' In the past, I think that learning occurred more incidentally. Specific activities weren't planned. This helped me be much more planful about academics in my activities."*

> **Vicki:** *"It was helpful to think about academic areas separately because sometimes I forget. This way I could ask myself, 'What am I doing? Is this math? Is this reading?' I still get lots of pressure from families concerned about whether their children are learning the alphabet and pre-reading and pre-math skills. I might start showing my planning frameworks to them so they can see the close attention I am paying to academics for their children."*

> **Valerie:** *"I think it's great to put academic activities down right on the plan. Now, I always include a science experiment, a special math activity, and a specific writing opportunity for the children."*

Challenging Children's Thinking

On the second sheet of the framework is a box labeled "Challenging Children's Thinking." Here is another place that teachers can highlight learning opportunities in their classrooms. Within the misunderstanding of "academic" versus "non-academic" curricula is the idea that in a developmentally appropriate, exploration-based curriculum, children are not being challenged to understand more complex concepts or achieve higher skill levels.

In individualizing curriculum, it is essential that teachers recognize the children's level of development in a variety of skills and challenge them to continue to grow and achieve higher levels of development. Challenge is indeed a part of best practices. But the trick is to identify the amount of challenge that is just right for each child so that she continues to try the new skill or understand the new concept. If the challenge is too hard, the child may give up, feel overwhelmed, get frustrated, or withdraw. If the challenge is too easy, the child may become uninterested, bored, misbehave, or give up and withdraw as well.

The "Challenging Children's Thinking" box on the framework is a place for a teacher to write down individual challenges that she is offering to different children, or group challenges that she is using to entice children to interact differently with materials or with others in the group.

Sue focused on a topic of interest to her students in early fall. As they began to notice leaves changing color, they started announcing their ideas as to why this color change occurred. One child persuaded many in the class that he knew the answer: the rain was washing off the green paint on the leaves, showing their real colors. Sue brought in many leaves of different colors and set up a challenge in her classroom. She provided a tub of soapy water and invited children to wash the leaves and change their colors. When the children realized that the colors were not changing with washing, she challenged them to consider some other reasons why leaves change colors.

Challenges can be identified for individual children as well. A child who counts to twenty can be challenged to count higher. A child who can almost tie her shoe successfully can be challenged to master the last few steps in the process. A child who is making shapes that look like letters at the writing center can be challenged to make those shapes more accurately. A child who always plays alone can be challenged to play with a small group of children. Individual challenges are also included in the "Individual Adjustments" portion of the planning framework and may overlap each other. Both challenging children's thinking and individual adjustments contribute to the individualizing of the curriculum, making certain that a "one size fits all" approach is not used.

Here are some examples of what teachers have written in the "Challenging Children's Thinking" boxes for all of the children in their classroom.

Challenging Children's Thinking

Can anyone build our school with blocks?

Gayle's Plan

Challenging Children's Thinking

How many colors can you sort? Are there other ways to sort the buttons or bottle caps?

Valerie's Plan

Challenging Children's Thinking

Who can look at our bird books and figure out what kind of bird is building her nest outside our classroom? Do we have her bird call on our tape?

Mrs. Chang's Plan

On the next page are some examples of what teachers have written in the "Challenging Children's Thinking" boxes for individual children in their classroom.

Challenging Children's Thinking

Brittany - writing her name - she's almost there!

Jony - counting with 1-1 past 4

Andrew - sitting thru a story

Genevieve's Plan

Challenging Children's Thinking

Jon, David, Mario & Peng - can you build a ramp together with blocks so the cars go as far across the room as possible?

Suzi - be a special friend to our new girl, Alicia

Marla - zipping her coat

Mark's Plan

Challenging Children's Thinking

Maria & Julio - can you count to 20? Higher? (Check 1-1 correspondence)

Joey - cutting with scissors

If problems arise with Juliet, Sofia, & Linda - help them problem-solve at the peace table

Luis' Plan

Focus on Teaching: The University Course Catalog Approach

Newspaper editors, community members, families seeking quality programs, and early childhood teachers have miscommunicated with one another about this issue of academics for young children. When early childhood programs describe their curricula as "play-based," many people outside the field interpret that to mean learning is not part of the curriculum. To help counteract this misinterpretation, I suggest that early childhood professionals consider describing the imbedded academics in our programs using terminology that sounds like it came from a university course catalog.

For example, in any quality early childhood classroom structured for exploration of a rich classroom environment, children are exposed to the concepts of physics, chemistry, meteorology, biology, botany, and anatomy. When children build and construct with blocks in the block area, they are routinely experimenting with gravity and balance, force and mass, friction and momentum—all physical forces studied in physics. When children cook with teachers and observe changes to ingredients as they are mixed and heated, they are exploring the principles of chemistry. Daily weather observations are common in most early childhood classrooms. And seasonal changes are experienced with outdoor time and neighborhood walks. Biology and botany are included in studies of animals and plants. Children care for classroom pets and plants, visit farms and zoos, and learn more about insects and spiders. They may plant a center garden or flowerbed.

Human anatomy is always included in any classroom of young children because their own bodies fascinate them. Classroom teachers recognize this fascination and plan activities that capture the children's interest. Teachers help children learn more about health and nutrition, the importance of exercise, and the functions of various body parts and organs.

Using the university course catalog terms of physics and anatomy can help parents and community members recognize that the concepts of many scientific disciplines are included in the early childhood curriculum. They are included in an exploratory, active learning environment through a variety of hands-on activities. A lecture, followed by paperwork, quizzes, and tests are not the formats in which these concepts are taught. The emphasis in preschool classrooms is on the children developing observation and analysis skills, making predictions, problem solving, and experimenting. These are all scientific skills that will serve them well as they mature into older grades and are ready for the introduction of more vocabulary and abstract concepts.

Language Arts, Math, and Social Studies

Terminology from the other major content areas that form the basis of academics—language arts, math, and social studies—can also be used in preschool programs. Here are lists of concepts and skills that are imbedded in quality early childhood curricula from the core academic areas of language arts, math, and social studies. These concepts may not sound like they come from a university course catalog as our science list did. However, you may recognize terms that are common in the elementary grades. By no means are these lists complete. What concepts would you add?

Pam: *"I really struggled providing challenges to children's thinking. But I ended up really liking this aspect of the framework. I would pose challenges like adding hollow blocks to our block area, and asking the children 'What can you make with these?' Or, when our thematic study was about transportation, I posed the challenge, 'What can you make that you can ride in.' One time, I put out a train set with no tracks, and asked the children, 'How can you make tracks?' Another time, I posed the question, 'How can you find out whether things have wheels?' We looked in our classroom library and took a trip to the school library to get more resources about things with wheels. I've learned that some of the kids really respond to these challenges. It makes me think about posing questions to kids more regularly and consciously."*

Language Arts

- Listening
- Reading comprehension
- Phonics/awareness of sounds
- Speaking
- Vocabulary development
- Knowledge of books and print

Math

- Sorting and categorizing (ordering and patterning)
- Counting and quantity
- Geometry and spatial relationships
- Problem solving
- Measurement
- Representing mathematical information

Social Studies

- Families
- Getting along with others
- Community

Where do these academics occur in a classroom? If there are no lectures, if the approach emphasizes children as active learners, how are academics addressed? We can all easily answer this question if we take the time to analyze the daily routines in our classrooms and to reconsider the way we write lesson or activity plans.

In all programs for young children, daily routines incorporate reading, math, social studies, and science. The following daily schedule of a typical preschool classroom is listed alongside possible academic goals for each and every part of the day. The goals are written in the university course catalog approach to help others see how learning is at the core of everything we do with preschoolers.

Sample Daily Schedule for a Preschool Half-Day

8:00–8:25 A.M. Arrival Time

The children put away their backpacks and coats and go to tables where hands-on materials are available (paper and instruments for writing or drawing such as markers or pencils; small manipulatives for constructing, such as Legos building blocks; and playdough).

Academics: speaking, vocabulary development, getting along with others, taking care of our community (namely, the classroom)

8:25–8:45 A.M. Large Group Time
The children join in movement games, songs, and finger plays, then listen to discussions and stories before planning for the day.
   Academics: listening, reading comprehension, phonics/awareness of sounds (such as rhyming songs), counting and quantity (such as counting when taking attendance), biology (such as reading a story about frogs), our community (such as learning to take turns and respect others in the group)

8:45–10:00 A.M. Work or Activity Time
The children choose among a variety of learning areas and may be asked to join in a small group activity led by a teacher for approximately 10–15 minutes of this time.
   Academics: physics (balance, gravity, mass, force), measurement, and problem solving at the block area; chemistry in the cooking activity (teacher-led small group); knowledge of books and print at the class library; our families at dramatic play; sorting and categorizing at manipulatives

10:00–10:15 A.M. Cleanup Time
The children help clean up the entire classroom.
   Academics: sorting and categorizing, counting and quantity (the children place items back in their baskets and on shelves); our community (the children work together for a common end)

10:15–10:30 A.M. Snack Time
The children converse and eat snack.
   Academics: speaking, vocabulary development, general health

10:30–11:00 A.M. Outdoors
The children engage in a variety of large-muscle activities, outdoors if weather permits.
   Academics: botany and meteorology (explore plants and weather outdoors); general health (run, jump, and play); counting and quantity (wait for turns on the bikes or swings)

11:00–11:15 A.M. Prepare to Go Home
Get materials, backpacks, coats, and so forth. Review the day's activities and make plans for tomorrow.
   Academics: our community (cleanup); listening and comprehension (review and plan)

11:15 A.M. Dismissal

Such banal activities as lining up to go outside (learning the concept of ordering—first, second, third) or setting the table for snack (children put one-to-one correspondence into action) incorporate academic learning. The learning areas in the environment incorporate academics as well. At the dramatic play area, the teachers can see a child's movement toward abstract thinking as he pretends that the block held up to his ear is a telephone. The teachers can witness the development of the children's oral language skills as they act out scenes, and can learn more about their understanding of family life as the scenes of mommy, daddy, and baby proceed.

The children's scientific observation skills are in practice at the sensory table or art area in such activities as mixing colors, pouring water over waterwheels, describing the feel of cornstarch mixed with water, and predicting what might happen if water is added to sand. In the classroom library, the teachers give the children opportunities to retell familiar stories from the pictures in the book, encouraging awareness of the printed word and development of vocabulary. The teachers can also assess the children's comprehension.

Yes to Academics!

Academics, even rigorous academics, are indeed incorporated into early childhood programs. When a community member or a potential new family asks, "Are you an academic program?" my response is an enthusiastic, "Yes!" Then I explain how academics occur in this program. Skill-and-drill activities are not evident. Academic learning is playful and exploratory. The children contribute their own ideas, use their own problem-solving strategies, and pursue their own interests. Teachers skillfully weave in the goals and objectives of traditional academics as they build on what the children can do and challenge them to try new things. Teachers recognize that we must have expectations and standards in our programs. But they also know the nature of learning at this age. Because teachers use play as a way to build children's success does not mean the curriculum is neither rigorous nor academic. It means that it is appropriate for the children.

When teachers incorporate academics into the curriculum, they raise the level of accountability. By including academic terminology (even university course catalog vocabulary) in the planning framework, teachers are reminding themselves and communicating to others that indeed they are thinking first and foremost about learning. By thinking about goals, objectives, and challenges, and by writing them down each week, teachers are helping others witness how much they know about their children's growth and development and how hard they are working to support and challenge each child.

chapter 6

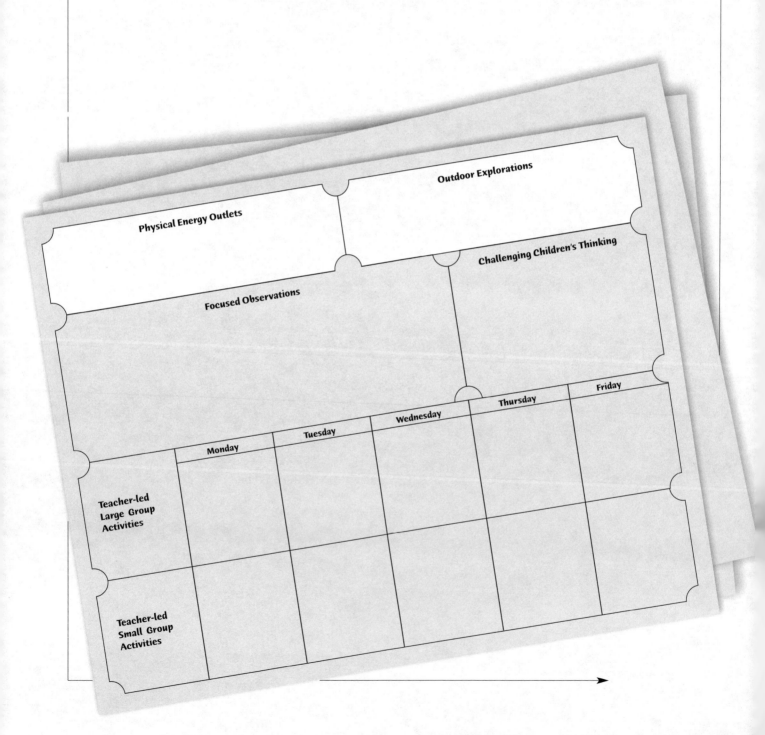

Physical Energy Outlets and Outdoor Explorations

Young children are movers and shakers, wigglers and doers. They have energy to burn and the desire to try out things actively for themselves. They are risk takers, exploring their own capabilities and not always recognizing safety issues.

They are not passive receptors or good listeners. Their primary mode of taking in new information is not by watching demonstrations or listening to lectures. Instead, they are active learners. They are builders and constructors. They are climbers and runners. They are scientists experimenting with new and exciting ways to use materials. They are artists and dancers, exploring their own creativity and freedom in space, figuring out just how to express their unique selves.

Young children do not express their feelings in words as much as behavior. Their bodies are their primary communication source. Their words and vocabulary have not caught up yet to the range of intense emotions they experience in short periods of time, especially when dealing with a classroom of other children their age.

Teachers in good preschool programs know very well that young children need a number of outlets for their energy and emotional expressions. And they know that a brief recess or outdoor time will not provide enough release to meet children's needs. Therefore, they make sure that the classroom environment provides opportunities for movement, exploration, and hands-on manipulation of objects. They carefully evaluate their daily schedule to make sure that sitting and listening times are briefer than times for hands-on activities.

Physical Energy Outlets

On the Focused Early Learning planning framework is a box labeled "Physical Energy Outlets." Here, each week, teachers identify what specific equipment, materials, opportunities, and activities they will provide in their classroom to help children express themselves physically. These outlets might be already included in the daily choices of learning areas in the classroom. For example, the block and dramatic play areas are often very physical areas. Circle time often includes dancing and movement activities. Highlighting these existing physical activities on the planning framework may be all that is needed some weeks.

Here are some examples of the planning teachers have done for physical energy outlets in their classrooms.

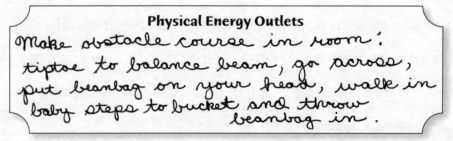

Physical Energy Outlets

Make obstacle course in room: tiptoe to balance beam, go across, put beanbag on your head, walk in baby steps to bucket and throw beanbag in.

Pam's Plan

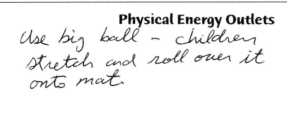

Physical Energy Outlets

Use big ball — children stretch and roll over it onto mat.

Vee's Plan

Physical Energy Outlets

Go to gym & use hoops & beanbags — throwing, jumping, hopping

Valerie's Plan

Focus on Teaching: Choosing Physical Energy Outlets

Recognizing that more opportunities to expend energy may be necessary for preschool children, many teachers will want to plan for specific physical activities in addition to those embedded in everyday routines. Here are some ideas for equipment, materials, and activities that could be provided as outlets in the classroom. By no means are these lists all-inclusive. What else have you found that helps children burn energy and express themselves physically?

Equipment

- Rocking boat/stair climber
- Large exercise ball
- Indoor climber or a loft
- Crawling tunnel
- Puppet stage and puppets
- Woodworking bench
- Water/sand table

Materials

- Scarves for dancing to music
- Plastic ABC mats (or ABC rug) for walking/jumping/tiptoeing the ABCs
- Plastic bowling set
- Beanbags and target

- Foam balls for playing catch and rolling games
- Balloons (Who can keep theirs from touching the floor? Can you hit it to a friend so he can catch it?)
- Bubbles (Can you stomp them? Can you catch them? Whose went the highest? Whose is the biggest?)

Activities

- Create an obstacle course in the classroom (Tiptoe for five steps, turn around and walk backwards for four steps, crawl under the table, climb over the chair, jump up and down three times, clap your hands, and give me a hug.)
- Paint hands and feet
- Trace our bodies on large pieces of paper and decorate/color them
- Build block structures to act out stories (such as the bridge for "Three Billy Goats Gruff," the three pigs' houses, the three bears' chairs and beds)
- Play "I Spy" (Look around the classroom for something yellow, for circles, for your name.)
- Play group games (such as "Simon Says," "Doggie, Doggie Who's Got Your Bone?" "Duck-Duck-Goose," and "Mother, May I?")
- Add variations to relay races (Hop like a kangaroo, crawl like a snake, roll like a roly-poly bug, tiptoe, walk backwards, hop on one foot, or even carry water or a plastic egg on a plastic spoon.)
- Play "People Sorting" (The "sorter" asks specific children to come up to the front of the group because they have some visible characteristic in common—all have tie shoes, brown hair, wear glasses, are girls, and so on. The group guesses what the common feature is.)
- Play cooperative games such as "Cows and Ducks," "Knee to Knee," "Cooperative Musical Chairs," or "Help" *(See p. 77 at the end of this chapter for game directions.)*

Much of the equipment, materials, and activities I have listed above have traditionally been seen as "rainy day activities." I am proposing that we offer such activities on a daily basis, making sure that the children get the opportunity to have physical activity both indoors and out every day. If they have energy to burn, why not provide outlets so that they can settle down more easily when they need to?

Settling Children Down

I am not saying that the classroom should be the equivalent of the outdoor play area. Children also need quiet activities and opportunities to concentrate on tasks that are more cognitive or fine motor in nature. If a teacher provides physical energy outlets in the classroom, he will want to make sure that he balances those outlets with a quiet reading corner and listening station; soothing art activities such as painting with shaving cream or water colors; cognitively demanding challenges in puzzles and math manipulatives; and soft cuddling opportunities with pets, stuffed animals, and baby dolls. For children who are drawn repeatedly to the physical, teachers will want to help them calm down by perhaps limiting their time on the climbing structure or with bubbles or balloons, and then helping them choose another, more sedentary activity.

Young children do not always balance the use of their own physicality and energy well. We, as adults, must guide them in finding that balance. Providing physical energy outlets and recognizing when a child is ready to move on to a more quiet activity are ways we can maintain reasonable classroom control and still recognize the needs of young children.

Planning Outdoor Explorations

Quality early childhood programs offer outdoor physical activity on a daily basis (weather permitting, of course). Young children's growing bodies are developing muscle control and need to expend energy and to experience fresh air and the delights of nature. Teachers should include recess or outdoor time whenever weather permits.

The framework offers a box for teachers to record their plans for outdoor explorations. Planning and thinking about what outdoor opportunities to provide is truly beneficial to the children. Teachers also may feel that outdoor time is more purposeful and less chaotic.

I am not recommending that the time spent outdoors should be totally teacher-directed. Freedom to run and run until your lungs ache from the fresh, cool air flowing through them is too important for young children. Using muscles in new ways and taking risks in climbing or swinging cannot be "taught." Sitting under a tree and watching the clouds go by through the leaves or observing the ants around their hole is a precious individual moment with nature in which no one, not even a teacher, should intervene.

Here are some examples of teachers' plans for outdoor explorations using the framework.

Mary: *"Having a space for physical energy outlets is a good way to emphasize the importance of that in an early childhood classroom and helps me focus on that as well. I'm consciously trying to build in those outlets throughout the day."*

Vicki: *"This section made me think about physical activity that is not just outside. Sometimes, we would plan to do the 'Hokey Pokey' or bounce a ball inside. I could see this would be very important for a full-day classroom. And, next year, my class will be mostly young three-year-olds. I can see that physical energy outlets will be really important for them!"*

Valerie: *"I do sensorimotor skills regularly with my children and incorporated those into the physical energy outlets. Last year, I could do them right in the classroom. This year I'll have to go to the gym, or to the hallway downstairs, because my new classroom is very small."*

Pam: *"My physical energy outlets tend to be more spontaneous than planned, so I don't always write something down in this part of the framework. For example, if we read a story about animals, then the transition from that story to centers will be to move like your favorite animal. I do use this as a plan for bad weather when we can't go outside. Then, I'll set up the bowling set or create an indoor obstacle course."*

Outdoor Explorations

Take parachute outdoors.

Pam's Plan

Outdoor Explorations

Look for leaves, collect seeds and insects as well.

Linde's Plan

Outdoor Explorations

Take paint easels out. Take blanket & basket of books for reading

Gayle's Plan

Focus on Teaching: Changing Possibilities Outdoors

Planning for changing possibilities outdoors can enrich the experiences inherent at recess time. Introducing new equipment, materials, or activities can make every outdoor time an adventure. With changing possibilities, children may try more new things or stay interested longer. Teachers are providing a sense of some structure to a time that is ripe with freedom for exploration and physical expression.

Here are some ideas for equipment, materials, and activities that can be added to the outdoor area and recorded on the planning framework. The assumption underlying all of the lists is that most programs' outdoor areas minimally contain some running space and climbing equipment. Again, by no means are these suggestions all-inclusive. What else has worked successfully for you?

Equipment
- Bikes, wagons, or carts
- Climbing tunnel
- Large exercise ball
- Balls in different sizes, targets
- Woodworking bench
- Sand/water table
- Gardening tools

Materials
- Streamers or scarves for feeling/seeing the wind at work
- Bubbles
- Spray bottles filled with water for painting the pavement or walls
- Paintbrushes and buckets of water for painting
- Magnifying glasses and books about insects
- Sidewalk chalk
- Small cars and trucks for the sandbox
- Jump ropes
- Plastic-can stilts
- Hoops of various sizes
- Binoculars for watching birds or clouds
- Tape recorder for taping bird songs or outdoor noises
- Dress-up clothes for dramatic play (Avoid long skirts and high-heel shoes.)

Activities
- Read under a tree (Sit on a blanket or plastic mat.)
- Wash the baby dolls or dishes in the water table
- Wash the classroom chairs and tables
- Paint outdoors; use the easel
- Carefully observe ice cubes as they melt
- Adopt a tree; check on it regularly in each season
- Go on a nature scavenger hunt: collect leaves (different colors, shapes), nuts, rocks, and feathers
- Count and categorize the trucks that drive by (How many cement trucks? Dump trucks? Tow trucks?)
- Do texture rubbings with crayon; use paper, pavement, cement, fence, wall, slide, and so on
- Organize a driver's license bureau for all bike riders; have "police officers" enforce traffic rules, check licenses, and give tickets

- Do an obstacle course: climb up the slide and go down the slide, run over to the sandbox, walk around the edge, jump through the hoop, and give me a hug
- Organize group games: "Red Light, Green Light," "Duck-Duck-Goose," "Mother, May I?"
- Run relay races; add variations such as running, jumping, walking like various animals
- Play catch and rolling games
- Have a picnic—eat snack outside!

The possibilities are endless, aren't they? The goal, however, is the same: children running, jumping, climbing, hiding, swinging, digging, and taking advantage of the basic equipment, space, and freedom in the outdoor area. The suggested equipment, materials, and activities listed above are offered in addition to the basic setup.

Thinking about and planning for physical energy outlets in the classroom is an important task that will enhance an early childhood classroom. Even with the most careful plans, flexibility and responsiveness are necessary as well. How many times have teachers talked about how "squirrelly" their children were today? Or, asked, "Is it a full moon? My kids sure are acting crazy!" Identifying some ways to provide outlets for physical energy each week, and being prepared to offer spontaneous physical activities when needed, will make preschool and kindergarten teachers' jobs much easier and successful in the long run. By doing so, teachers are recognizing and celebrating the essence of young children, rather than working against their very natures.

Pam: *"Including outdoor explorations on the framework made me think, and made me feel guilty, about bringing materials outside and planning more for outdoor time rather than just letting it happen."*

Reflecting on Physical Energy Outlets and Outdoor Explorations

Remember to reflect on how well both of these areas are going when engaging in the reflection process. Are the physical energy outlets this week feeling out of control? Maybe more adult supervision for that area was needed. Or, perhaps fewer children should participate at one time. Did any children wander outdoors or appear to not engage in any one activity? Maybe it's time to bring out something from indoors. Many teachers find that bringing out an easel and paints, or the water table and babies to wash, can spark interest in the children who are not interested in the usual climbing and swinging equipment.

Here are some examples of teachers' reflections about these active areas and the plans they made in response.

Physical Energy Outlets

BALLOON CATCH GOT OUT OF CONTROL — HARD FOR MARNI & I TO SUPERVISE.

Luis' Reflection

Physical Energy Outlets

SET UP PLASTIC BOWLING SET — MARNI GIVE INSTRUCTIONS TO THOSE BOWLING. THEN FLOAT AROUND CLASSROOM KEEPING AN EYE ON BOWLERS.

Luis' Plan

Outdoor Explorations

Last week "exploring ways our body can move" was too vague. Kids didn't know what to do.

Vee's Reflection

Outdoor Explorations

How many different ways can you move like an animal? Animal relay races.

Vee's Plan

How to Play the Cooperative Games

I learned these games attending a variety of workshops on cooperative games over the years. The goal is that everyone wins—there are no losers. Some open space is needed for each game.

Cows and Ducks

Tell the children that they must decide inside their mind what kind of animal they are going to be—either a cow or a duck. The only way anyone will know which animal they are is by the sound they will make. Once they start making the sound, they need to find all of the other children who are making the same sound as their animal and get together in a group. "Ready, set, go!" Once the two groups have formed, have them line up facing each other and analyze their size by counting, comparing lengths, or whatever. The game can be played again and again with the same animals, or with other animal pairs that will make for interesting and fun sounds and organizing in groups. Let the children suggest such pairs!

Knee to Knee

Each child has a partner. The caller (begin with the teacher, then have children take turns) announces a body part in this fashion, "Knee to knee." Each pair of children must stand knee to knee. Try elbows, shoulders, pinky fingers, backs, and so on.

Cooperative Musical Chairs

This game is played as traditional musical chairs is played, except no one is ever out. Instead, any child that does not have a seat, poses it as a problem for the whole group to solve. "How can we help 'so-and-so' to be able to sit somewhere?" Let the children offer to share chairs or have someone sit on their lap or sit next to them. Be prepared for lots of giggles!

Help

This is my favorite indoor cooperative game. It really settles children down and helps them to be more sensitive to others' needs. It can go on for quite a long time with some groups.

You will need tissues such as Kleenex separated to one thickness. Each child gets a tissue, which is then carefully placed on each child's head. Each child may walk around the room as long as the tissue is in place on her head (no holding on allowed!). If the tissue falls off, the child is frozen, and cannot move until a friend is kind enough to gently place the tissue back on top of the head. Then, the child who was frozen can move again. If the tissue falls off the child who was helping, that child is also frozen until someone comes and helps. The children may not call out for help; instead, their friends have to pay close attention and be ready to help any friend in need.

chapter 7

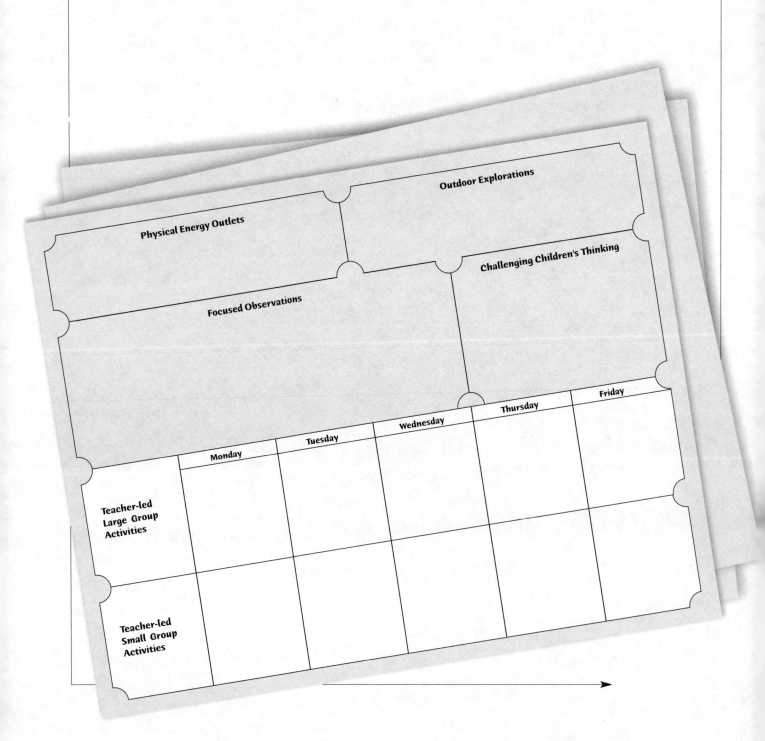

Balancing Child Choice with Teacher-Led Activities

In good preschool classrooms, teachers recognize that offering choices brings about more participation and engagement in activities. Young children do not respond well to constantly being told what to do. As Erik Erikson identified, they are in the stage of initiative—trying things out for themselves. Their developing independence and movement toward greater competence propels them to reject constant direction from the adults in their lives.

Yet, it is not complete freedom from adult guidance that they seek. Children trust adults to provide reasonable choices within the safety of adult guidance. In an early childhood classroom, children rarely choose, from among all imaginable choices, to do anything they wish. Instead, the possibilities from which they can choose are carefully planned and facilitated by teachers.

Teachers take into consideration both the ages and developmental levels of the children. They consider the children's personalities, dispositions to learning, past experiences, and cultural backgrounds. Never is any part of the day unplanned by the teacher. The classroom organization and use of time are structured. However, within this structure, teachers enable the children to make choices about which activities they will do and when, different ways in which they will use the materials, and with whom they will interact while they do so. Also, within this careful planning, a teacher provides some activities where she is the leader and initiator, not the child. The tricky part is to find just the right balance between child choice and teacher-led activities.

Teacher-Led Large Group Time

On the frameworks, there is a section entitled "Teacher-Led Large Group Activities." This area is where teachers can list the songs and finger plays they plan to use for group time. Discussion topics, demonstrations, or stories can also be written here. In some classrooms, teachers include daily routines such as taking attendance, identifying classroom helpers, looking at a calendar, and making plans for the day. All of these routines can be written on the planning form each week—or they can be included in a more generic term, "Daily Routines." The only caution about the latter is if a substitute teacher is ever using the framework in the absence of the teacher. In that case, explanations of daily routines should be somewhere in a substitute teacher folder. Here are examples of Valerie's plans for large groups.

	Monday	Tuesday	Wednesday	Thursday	Friday
Teacher-led Large Group Activities	"Hokey Pokey" "Head, Shoulders, Knees & Toes" Daily Routines Build flannel board body with parts Read "Here Are My Hands"	Play "Knee to Knee" "Where is Thumbkin" Daily Routines Read "Maisy Dresses Up"	Hap Palmer "Shake Something" "Touch" Daily Routines Body Parts Mix Up (Flannel board)	"Hokey Pokey" "Knee to Knee" "Thumbkin" Daily Routines Read & Act Out "I Can Do That"	No Class

Valerie's Plan Week 1

Notice how each day, Valerie begins her large group with an active song and some kind of movement, which pulls the group together. She then progresses to calmer activities and finger plays. Daily routines are followed by either a large group learning activity or a story. The children know exactly what to expect each day as her routine remains the same. Later in this chapter, we'll analyze large group planning in more depth and discuss whether it is even necessary to plan a large group time every day.

Teacher-Led Small Group Time

Sometimes, preschool teachers lead small group activities. These may include work with specific skills such as counting, writing, shape recognition, or sorting and classifying. They may include producing something such as an "All about Me" book or artwork using coffee filters and food dye. For safety purposes, many teachers do science experiments or cooking activities in small groups, where they can supervise the children closely. It's often easier to keep the children's attention in a small group, since small group times allow teachers to pay closer attention to individual children and focus on their growing skills and abilities. Assessing their progress is also more easily done in the small group setting.

On the planning framework, there is a box to list plans for teacher-led small groups. Keeping the purpose of small group clear and establishing time limits will ensure that the children gain from the experience rather than just pass time. If a specific project, such as an experiment or cooking is involved, the small group time can last until the project is completed. If the activity involves working with specific skills, the teacher can be sensitive to how long the children stay interested and actively engaged.

For example, if the goal is to work with the children on sorting and classifying small manipulatives, a teacher may want to plan several activities that will encourage the children to demonstrate sorting and classifying skills in a variety of ways. The following plan for such a teacher-led small group might be written on the framework:

> "Sorting/Classifying: colored tiles on colored plates; stringing beads in patterns on necklaces; sorting bottle caps and buttons."

The variety of materials allows the teacher to keep the children's interest in the small group activity for a longer period. This helps to develop children's attention spans, and gives them the opportunity to work more fully with the concept at hand. In the process, the teacher gains more information about each child's understanding of the concepts involved.

Here is an example of Linde's plan for teacher-led small group.

	Monday	Tuesday	Wednesday	Thursday	Friday
Teacher-led Small Group Activities	Throughout the week, Linde will lead leaf activities — leaf sorting, matching, classifying; leaf rubbings + cut them out (fine motor); leaf painting and making prints.				

Linde's Plan Week 1

Using the Reflection Framework

The reflection framework or general reflection form can be a way to analyze how successful your teacher-led large and small group times are going. Here you can note how long the children stayed engaged in the activity. Writing down which particular children had trouble sitting through a story or waiting their turn to stir the cookie batter can guide you to a better plan, both for the group as a whole and for that individual child. Here are some examples of ways that teachers have planned and reflected about their teacher-led activities and changed their approaches either for the whole group or for individual children.

	Monday	Tuesday	Wednesday	Thursday	Friday
Teacher-led Large Group Activities	Hokey Pokey was hard because so many children don't know right from left. Need more settling time to calm down – finger plays? Quiet games? Before story reading. Good body parts recognition throughout the week – even ankles & wrists.				

Valerie's Reflection Week 1

	Monday	Tuesday	Wednesday	Thursday	Friday
Teacher-led Large Group Activities	"Knee to Knee Game" "Wiggles" "My Thumbs Go Up" Daily Routines Read "It Looked Like Spilled Milk"	→ → → Read "Jump, Frog, Jump"	Hap Palmer: "Shake Something" "Touch" Children choose a favorite story	Play "Simon Says" "Give Yourself A Hug" Re-read "Spilled Milk" Children predict & read along	No Class

Valerie's Plan Week 2

	Monday	Tuesday	Wednesday	Thursday	Friday
Teacher-led Small Group Activities	The children are so interested in animals – the leaves lost their interest as the week went on. Sorted and classified 3 types of leaves: Erik, Yesenia, Diana, Willy, Alex, Juan, Vanessa and Miriam.				

Linde's Reflection Week 1

	Monday	Tuesday	Wednesday	Thursday	Friday
Teacher-led Small Group Activities	Animal Classification Cards —————————————————→ Play Bingo, Matching, Memory & Go Fish Discuss and name animals to develop vocabulary in English and Spanish				

Linde's Plan Week 2

Focus on Teaching: Balancing Child Choice with Teacher-Led Activities

If you notice that the children are not staying engaged in your teacher-led groups for as long as you would like, look at how balanced your classroom opportunities are between child-chosen and teacher-led activities. The first step is to look at the whole schedule for the preschool day. The focus of the activities throughout the day (or half-day, as the case may be) will vary between the teacher as the initiator, and the children as the initiators. In teacher-led activities, the children tend to play a more passive role. They are the receivers of information, ideas, or suggestions. In child-initiated activities, the children make decisions and take actions.

In her book, *Teacher* (1963), Sylvia Ashton-Warner talks about the need for children to have opportunities to "breathe out" and to "breathe in," or to experience activities for "output" or "intake." She defines "breathing out" as expressing oneself. Such expression can be by talking, singing, dancing, moving, writing, drawing, creating, or building. Ashton-Warner even includes crying, quarrelling, daydreaming, and loving as "output" or "breathing out" activities. She defines "breathing in," on the other hand, as taking in new information: listening, learning a new concept, watching a demonstration, pondering, or thinking. This can be tied directly to providing choices for children. When the children are the initiators, they are "breathing out." When the teachers are the initiators, the children are in the "breathing in" mode. The critical point Ashton-Warner makes is this: Children must first be given opportunities to breathe *out* before they are ready to breathe *in*.

Ashton-Warner sees the daily schedule in a classroom as a "daily rhythm" that flows from breathing out activities to breathing in activities. She says flowing with this daily rhythm, "The teacher is at last with the stream and not against it: the stream of children's inexorable creativeness" (p. 93). If breathing out precedes breathing in, children have had an opportunity to expend both physical and creative energy before they are asked to sit and be quiet. They have also had time to express and process any urgent feelings or experiences with which they came into the classroom that day. They are more ready to take in information from others, to listen to a story, or to follow directions.

Take a look at the following daily schedule and think about its daily rhythm. Notice where you see opportunities for the children to "breathe out" versus "breathe in." Does "breathing out" usually precede "breathing in"? The classroom routines of cleanup, getting ready for snack, or going home probably are neither output or intake activities—they just are things that have to be done, aren't they?

Sample Daily Schedule for a Preschool Half-Day

8:00–8:25 A.M. Arrival Time
Children put away their backpacks and coats and go to tables where hands-on materials are available (greetings and conversation; writing and drawing; small manipulatives for constructing, such as Lego building blocks; and playdough). *Breathing out*

8:25–8:45 A.M. Large Group Time
Children join in movement games, songs, and finger plays *(breathing out)*, then listen to discussions and stories before planning for the day. *Breathing in*

8:45–10:00 A.M. Work or Activity Time
The children choose among a variety of learning areas and may be asked to join in a small group activity led by a teacher for approximately 10–15 minutes of this time. *More breathing out than anything; small group may be either breathing out or in*

10:00–10:15 A.M. Cleanup Time
The children help clean up the entire classroom.

10:15–10:30 A.M. Snack Time
The children converse and eat snack. *Breathing out*

10:30–11:00 A.M. Outdoors
The children engage in a variety of large-muscle activities, outdoors if weather permits. *Breathing out*

11:00–11:15 A.M. Prepare to Go Home
Get materials, backpacks, coats, and so forth. Review the day's activities and make plans for tomorrow.

11:15 A.M. Dismissal

In my own preschool classroom, I had to try different schedules before I figured out how best to balance the activities so that they flowed from self-expression to taking in new information. The children in my class arrived at various times across a fifteen-minute period. Initially, I thought that we should begin the day with a large group or circle time. I reasoned that such a group experience would help everyone settle down, and feel like part of the group right off. My plan was for the children to sit quietly while attendance was taken, a story was read, and plans were made for the day. All of these activities, according to Ashton-Warner, were breathing-in activities.

I tried this for a few weeks, asking the children who arrived first to sit and wait until their classmates arrived. The waiting was excruciating for those children! And, even for those who arrived later, the large group time was not successful. They all had stories about the previous evening to tell to me and their friends. Several of them had brought things to show to the class, and wanted to do so immediately. Wiggles and giggles, and a general need for movement and conversation were evident as I continually attempted to "shush" the children.

Looking at this situation from Ashton-Warner's perspective, I had not given the children an opportunity to breathe out as they began their school day. I changed the schedule so that arrival time was a prolonged period. As children arrived, they put away their knapsacks and coats, and chose among a variety of table activities (writing, manipulatives, drawing, and books). Conversation among the children was encouraged. My teaching assistant and I circulated among the children, greeting them, hearing their stories from home, admiring the objects they had brought to school, and encouraging their self-expression through the activities at hand. As new children arrived, they easily joined in at the tables. Enough time was allowed so that all the children had an opportunity to converse, write, or draw for at least ten minutes. Then, large group time was held. By this time, the children were ready to breathe in. The group time transition went more smoothly than it had. The children sat and listened with more ease.

An Effective Large Group Time

The younger the children, the less time in a day should be spent in teacher-led, breathing-in activities. Three-year-olds will need more breathing-out time than five-year-olds. What teacher-led activities should be planned, then?

At large group time, teachers are usually the focus. Children are expected to sit in a group and receive information about the day, listen to a story, and take turns participating by raising hands or waiting to make comments or ask questions. Teachers often hope that group time will help build community among the children, help children know one another better, give children experience in listening and following directions, develop reading comprehension skills, and give children an opportunity to experiment with turn-taking.

How long should large group time last? There is no magic number for three- to five-year-olds. However, there is a very clear point at which large group time should end—when the children no longer show interest!

That means large group time may vary in length from day to day. At the beginning of the year, it may be a much shorter experience than at the end of the year. On a day when the children are particularly calm, and the story is a class favorite, large group time may last longer than usual. As group time progresses, teachers must be alert to the body language of the children. Are they sitting quietly with little movement, or are there lots of wiggles? Are the children keeping their hands to themselves, or are many of them fiddling with their neighbors in some way? Are the children actively engaged in the activity or conversation, or are they looking around the room, asking when circle time will be done, or staring with little light in their eyes, as if they've given up until this "ordeal" is over? Teachers need to read these signals to determine when to end a group activity, even stopping a story midstream if necessary.

Some teachers choose not to do large group times at all. They feel that the goals of building community, developing listening and comprehension, turn-taking, and so on can be met in many other ways throughout the classroom day. Amethyst, Stephanie, and Christina had eighteen three- to five-year-olds in their classroom. They felt that large group time was not productive with that many children involved, and instead planned for small group activities at different times throughout the day to involve children in music and movement activities, daily routines, and story reading.

An effective group time is one that meets the needs of the children. Depending on the children and the program, a short group time, a longer group time, or even no group time at all can be successful. A teacher who understands this and plans group times that work for the children in her class is showing her sensitivity; she knows how best to plan for preschoolers.

One way to develop longer engagement in circle time activities is to apply the concepts of "breathing out" and "breathing in." Beginning large group time with songs and movement games that give the children the opportunity to express themselves physically helps them breathe out. Moving toward less and less physical activity helps the children get ready to breathe in and listen more attentively to discussions and stories.

Beginning large group time by calling the children together with movement songs, such as "The More We Get Together," grabs the children's attention, brings them into the circle, and lets them expend energy by moving their bodies.

> Oh, the more we get together, together, together,
> The more we get together, the happier we'll be.
> Move this way and that way and this way and that way.
> Oh, the more we get together, the happier we'll be.

Additional verses can be added using the children's names and allowing each of them to decide on a movement the class can replicate. These movements are all done standing up. The children might suggest raising their arms, swinging their legs, jumping up and down, or touching their toes.

> Andrea moves this way and Joseph moves that way,
> Yolanda moves this way and Ari moves that way.

Following such vigorous activity with a less vigorous movement song or game will lead the children to sit down quietly. For example, the following finger play begins with the children standing up, and ends with them sitting down.

> I wiggle my fingers, I wiggle my toes,
> I wiggle my elbows, I wiggle my nose,
> I get all of my wiggles out of me.
> And, then, I sit quiet, as quiet can be.

Now, the children may be more ready to participate in a discussion that requires listening and taking turns responding, or to listen to a story. If there are still some wiggles, add a sitting-down song or finger play with minimal movement (such as "Open, Shut Them" or "Eeensy, Weensy Spider"). These activities have progressed from "breathing out" (active, self-expression) to "breathing in" (quietly taking in new information). Many teachers report that this progression lengthens the attentiveness of children and increases the effectiveness of their large group times.

At the end of this chapter, I have included the words to several songs and finger plays. Some work best to call the children to group time or to dismiss them to the next activity. Others start with the children standing up, but end up with them sitting down. And, still others are meant to continue the quieting down process after the children are seated in the large group. Thanks to all of the teachers who have shared these songs, chants, and finger plays with me over the years.

Providing Child Choice in Exploring the Classroom Environment

In chapter 3, we discussed the many possibilities for children to try in a classroom environment. The question to consider now is, "How much of children's explorations should be based on their choices, and how much should be based on teacher suggestions or directions?" Again, the younger the child, the more the balance should be in favor of children's choices (within carefully teacher-planned sets of choices).

For preschoolers, the physical environment, as well as the rules and procedures of the classroom, provides a structure to the choices made. Many preschool teachers allow children to choose an exploration activity. They recognize that children often choose learning areas for good reasons: The area may represent a strength or interest for that child, may have opportunities to practice skills the child is trying to master, may be a playmate's favorite, or may have something the child has not tried before.

Letting the children figure out how long they want to stay with specific activities is another way of providing choice. Timing the children and making them rotate to different learning areas does not allow them the opportunity to make a plan and stick with it through completion. Adult agendas of "fifteen minutes at a center" limit children's engagement from an outside source. Many preschoolers are perfectly capable of staying with one activity for much longer than fifteen minutes, provided it is a self-chosen activity that really interests the child. When teachers remember that such engagement is an important learning goal for this age group, they can relax and not worry about the children not getting to every learning area each day. Instead, they can wonder at the intensity of a serious block builder who works cooperatively with friends over long periods of time and creates interesting structures that include symmetry and gravity-defying balance. Or they can marvel at the engagement of a socializer who spends many hours cooking and developing family scenarios in the dramatic play center.

Managing an active classroom full of children choosing activities sometimes involves limiting their choices. Children who throw sand at the sand table are not following the procedures for that learning area. A teacher can then step in, remind the child of the dangers of throwing sand, and watch for careful use of the materials. If the child continues to throw sand, the teacher may limit the child's choices by saying something such as, "I already discussed with you how we use the sand safely. I can see that you're having trouble doing so. You are showing me that you can no longer work at the sand table. Tomorrow, you can show me how you remember to use the sand safely. Now, you may choose to put together some puzzles or listen to a story on the headphones. Which would you like to do?" In this case, the teacher took away the choice of using the sand, and offered two other options from which the child could choose. This is one way of structuring children's choices.

Another way is to determine how many children at a time can work in a specific learning area. Many teachers report that limiting the number of children leads to fewer behavior problems and more positive engagement with the activities. When considering the perfect number of children in an area, these teachers pay attention to the following:

- The amount of square footage in the area (Young children often need a circle of personal space that is approximately the size of a hula hoop within which to function.)
- The number of materials available so that children can participate fully in the activity (If a game has four game cards, it's appropriate for only four children; if there are two easels, only two children can paint.)
- The number of chairs that will fit comfortably at a table (Six chairs at the art table means only six children in the art learning area.)

The procedure for making choices in these classrooms includes considering how many children are already present in an area and referring to some recognized sign that reminds everyone how many children can work in that area at any one time. Some teachers use choosing boards where children place their name card or photograph on hooks or in pockets that signify a learning area in the classroom. Some teachers use sign-in sheets posted around the classroom. In this way, children practice their writing skills while also learning to take turns and to wait for an opening in a favorite area.

Teachers are continually attempting to find just the right balance between choices for children and teacher-led activities. No matter what the age of the class, some days it may be wiser to offer fewer choices than others. For example, the day after a major celebration, such as Halloween, is often too chaotic for young children. A day of more restricted choices with quieter activities may bring about better behavioral results than a day of many loud, active choices. The opposite will be true on other days. If a teacher sees that children are wandering and not engaging in activities she has planned, or not paying attention to teacher-led discussions or stories, she may want to ask the children, "What would you like to do next?" She can give some possibilities for special choices that are not frequently available, such as Twister or dancing to music with scarves. Or she can listen carefully to the suggestions of the children and follow one or more of those. The balancing act is a daily event that must be paid careful consideration in the classroom.

Transition Songs, Chants, and Finger Plays

Calling to and Sending Away

Willoughby Wallaby Woo
Willoughby, wallaby wee, an elephant sat on me!
Willoughby, wallaby woo, an elephant sat on you!
Willoughby, wallaby w_____ (substitute child's name starting with a "w" sound).
An elephant sat on _____ (child's name).

Hicklety Picklety
Hicklety Picklety bumblebee, who can say their name for me?
_____ (child says name)!
Clap it! _____ (child's name)!
Shout it! _____ (child's name)!
Whisper it! _____ (child's name)!

Paw Paw Patch
Where oh where is little _____ (child's name)?
Where oh where is little _____ (child's name)?
Where oh where is little _____ (child's name)?
Way down yonder in the paw paw patch.
Picking up paw paws and putting them in *(her/his)* pocket.
Picking up paw paws and putting them in *(her/his)* pocket.
Picking up paw paws and putting them in *(her/his)* pocket.
Way down yonder in the paw paw patch.

Rich and Chocolaty
We love _____, she's rich and chocolaty.
Her mother *(or grandma, or uncle, or foster dad)* puts her in her milk for extra energy!

Chickee Chickee
Hey there _____ you're a real cool cat.
You've got a lot of this and a lot of that.
We all think that you are really neat.
So come on down and do the Chickee Chickee beat.
Hands up Chickee Chickee, Chickee Chickee.
Hands down Chickee Chickee, Chickee Chickee.
Boom Boom *(punch the air)* Chickee Chickee, Chickee Chickee.
Turn around Chickee Chickee, Chickee Chickee.

The More We Get Together

Oh the more we get together, together, together,
The more we get together, the happier we'll be.
There's _____, and _____, and _____ and _____.
Oh the more we get together, the happier we'll be.

If You Have on Red

If you have on red, stand up quick.
If you have on red, stand up quick.
If you have on red, stand up quick.
And take a bow *(or go wash your hands, or go get your coat on,
   or go choose your center, and so on)*.

Quieting Children Down

One, Two

One, two, what do we do?
Three, four, sit on the floor.
Five, six, our legs are fixed.
Seven, eight, our backs are straight.
Nine, ten, now let's begin!

Wiggles

I wiggle my fingers. I wiggle my toes.
I wiggle my elbows. I wiggle my nose.
I get all my wiggles out of me.
And then I sit quiet as quiet can be.

My Thumbs Go Up

*Sing this with words the first time, hum it the second time,
and the third time do hand motions only.*

My thumbs go up, up, up.
My thumbs go down, down, down.
My thumbs go out, out, out.
My thumbs go in, in, in.
My thumbs go round and round.

Hello Neighbor
Hello neighbor, what do you say?
It's going to be a happy day.
Greet your neighbor *(shake hands)* and boogie on down.
Give a little bump and turn around.
Hello neighbor, what do you say?
It's going to be a happy day.
Greet your neighbor *(shake hands)* and boogie on down.
Give a little bump and sit on the ground.

Clap, Clap, Clap
Clap, clap, clap your hands.
Stomp, stomp, stomp your feet.
Give yourself a great big hug because you are so neat.
Clap, clap, clap your hands.
Stomp, stomp, stomp your feet.
Give yourself a great big hug and then please have a seat.

Under the Spreading Chestnut Tree
With each verse, eliminate a word and do the action until you are only doing actions.

Under the spreading chestnut tree,
Under the spreading chestnut tree,
With my doggie on my knee, oh how happy we will be
Under the spreading chestnut tree.

Circle Time (to the tune of *Jingle Bells*)
Repeat, whispering the last line.

Tap your toes. Shake your head. Turn yourself around.
We're ready now for circle time so quietly sit down.

Friends
Repeat in American Sign Language.

Friends, friends, 1, 2, 3. All my friends are here with me.
You're my friend. You're my friend. You're my friend. You're my friend.
Friends, friends, 1, 2, 3. All my friends are here with me.

chapter 8

The Focused Early Learning Weekly Planning Framework

Date: _____ Teacher: _____

Child-led Exploration in the Rich Classroom Environment

- Blocks
- Art
- Sensory Table
- Library
- Dramatic Play
- Writing Center
- Manipulatives
- Ongoing Projects
- Scientific Inquiries
- Reading and Writing
- Math Moments
- Steps to Relationship Building
- Individual Adjustments

Following Children's Interests with Ongoing Projects/Studies

another way to provide choices for children is to plan activities that focus on interests they have demonstrated. In the field of early childhood education, many curricular approaches suggest specific ways to go about planning with children's interests in mind. These approaches include the Project Approach, emergent curriculum, and the Reggio Emilia approach. Sensitive and responsive teachers have always recognized the interests of the children in their classroom and incorporated activities spontaneously or in a carefully planned manner.

Every day, children express their interests—sometimes in a very blunt fashion. In my own classroom, I would sit down with the children to read a big book at large group time. I remember one hot May day, I wore open-toed sandals. We did some settling-in chants and finger plays to get ready to listen. Then I showed the cover of the book, discussed the author's name, and asked what the children predicted the book might be about. All of a sudden, Jessica called out, "Mrs. Gronlund, you have big toes!"

What happened to my story time? I could have said, "Jessica, be quiet. Let's not talk about that now. We're going to read this story." However, there would have been little cooperation from the four- and five-year-olds in the room. Instead, they all had gathered around to check out my toes! I decided to go with the flow. I closed the book, and suggested that we look at everyone's toes. We ended up with a series of foot activities that day—measuring foot and toe size, sorting and classifying types of shoes, and painting with our feet. Every activity tied to feet still met developmental goals of the program—so the fact that the focus changed from my original plans did not affect the quality of the curriculum for that day. Only the subject changed—in a spontaneous response to an expressed interest on the part of Jessica and all of the children.

Carefully planning a series of activities and investigations based on the children's interests is another way to organize curriculum. In chapter 3, we gave the example of a bird building a nest right outside Mrs. Chang's classroom. The teachers and the children were fascinated by the materials the bird was using and the progress she was making. To build on this fascination, the teachers planned a series of activities based on birds and nest building. Binoculars were provided to watch the bird more closely. Writing and drawing about observations was encouraged. Books about birds were added to the class library. Tapes of birdcalls were put in the listening center. Materials to build nests were placed in the sensory table. In this case, the teachers were able to plan around a spontaneous event.

Using the Planning Framework

On the planning framework is a box for recording ongoing projects. If a teacher knows he will be responding to an interest of the children, he writes that topic here. The specific activities may be written in the other portions of the planning framework (as in chapter 3 with the bird topic). Remember that not all areas of the classroom have to be coordinated with a project. It only makes sense to change areas that easily relate to the topic at hand. The classroom environment will offer plenty for the children to do in nonrelated learning areas.

Using the Reflection Framework

In using the framework for projects and studies, the most critical thing to do is to record how the children's interest in a topic arose (as in Mrs. Chang's bird nest) and what actually occurred with activities related to the topic. See Mrs. Chang's reflection frameworks on pp. 107–108: the first, as she noted the children's emerging interest; the second, as she reflected on the first week of the bird project. Also included on pp. 109–110 is her follow-up plan on the complete planning framework to continue and add some bird activities in response to the children's interest.

Teachers sometimes plan a project or topic of study based on their past experiences and knowledge of young children's interests. For example, preschool children are often interested in transportation. Yet, in planning for investigation of transportation, teachers find that they still have to be responsive to the specific direction the children take. In his preschool classroom, Mark organized materials around different kinds of transportation and provided a variety of activities for the children to engage in. As the class discussed different ways to get places—cars, trucks, trains, and airplanes—Jack announced proudly that his father was an airline pilot. Mark noticed that for several days, Jack and his friends organized chairs and "flew airplanes." As he reflected on the week, he noted the children's behavior on his reflection framework.

> **Ongoing Projects**
>
> Kids really got going on airplanes because Jack's dad is a pilot — they arranged chairs as a plane & "flew"!

Mark's Reflection

He decided to support and add to this interest and wrote plans for the next week accordingly. *(Mark's plan is on pp. 101–102.)* Notice that not every group activity (large or small) is about airplanes. You don't need to stretch every activity to fit a topic. Only plan for those that make sense and are easily accommodated.

Mark offered materials in the writing area so that the children could make tickets, and guided them in involving other children to be the passengers, ticket agents, and luggage handlers. He also invited Jack's dad in

> **Vicki:** *"Now, we're doing bugs and plants, both at the same time. The kids just love both of these topics. We could probably do them the whole year. However, most of the time our projects last two to three weeks."*

> **Diana:** *"Our whole classroom was a grocery store for awhile. Some kids played in ways I hadn't seen before—interacting more in the grocery store activities. Then, when the weather got warm, we did ocean. The kids loved going around in their bare feet!"*

> **Valerie:** *"I like a theme or topic that focuses some of the activities. In October, I did two weeks on 'Our Body' and 'Physical Me' with related activities at large and small group times."*

to tell the class more about his job. When he arrived in full pilot uniform, the children beamed. Jack smiled most of all. The interest in airplanes, pilots, and airports lasted for a long time in this classroom.

In this same program, Susie tried to interest her children in the topic of transportation. They half-heartedly built roads for toy cars and trucks and counted wheels on construction vehicles. She noted their unenthusiastic responses on her general reflection form. But, the children's eyes lit up and they became actively engaged when a flock of geese settled on the pond outside their classroom windows. This, too, was noted in Susie's reflections and included in her plans for the next week. See Susie's reflection and plan on pp. 103–105.

Susie wisely changed her focus from transportation to geese, and helped the children figure out ways to count and record the number of geese each day. She provided books on geese in the class library and took the children outdoors to observe the geese at the pond more closely. Notice that she did not attempt to change everything in the classroom to be associated with geese. The "show" was right outside the classroom windows on the pond!

These examples demonstrate truly emergent curriculum—teachers who responded to children's interests and were willing to adapt activities accordingly. Now, with the combination of reflection and planning frameworks, they have a record of what occurred for others to witness.

All five of the teachers who field-tested the framework have ongoing projects or thematic studies in their classrooms, and used this portion of the framework to document them. Then they wove the project or study throughout the total framework in specific activities. Look for their comments in sidebars on these pages.

Focus on Teaching: Choosing Good Topics for Study

In *Emergent Curriculum* (1994), Elizabeth Jones and John Nimmo remind us that "a thoughtful emergent curriculum does not require teachers to actively pursue all of the interests shown by the children. There are myriad ideas initiated by children in their play. Some are fleeting or momentary—exciting at the time but not the basis for prolonged engagement" *(p. 33)*. How does a teacher know which interests to follow up on? Jones and Nimmo suggest that "teachers need to assess the potential of any interest for in-depth learning by both the individual child and other members of the adult-child classroom community" *(p. 33)*.

The Focused Early Learning Weekly Planning Framework

Date: November 15, 2000 Teacher: Mark

Child-led Exploration in the Rich Classroom Environment

Blocks
Build an airport & act out planes arriving, taking off

Dramatic Play
Act out airport ticket counter; plane with chairs; suitcases to pack and unpack

Manipulatives
Manipulate & solve problems with marble run and gears

Reading and Writing
Take photos of our airport & plane dramatic play — make a book with the children dictating words

Art
Car paintings; draw with markers

Sensory Table
Experiment with texture of shaving cream; write name or shapes

Library
Look at & listen to books on planes, airports, pilots, travel & other transportation

Writing Center
Make airplane tickets

Ongoing Projects
Transportation — airplanes & pilots

Math Moments
Count wheels on various types of transportation — using toy models & pictures

Scientific Inquiries
Make paper airplanes

Individual Adjustments
Help Jesse with fine motor tasks.
Give Graham & Molly earlier reminders for transitions.

Steps to Relationship Building
Invite Jack's Dad in uniform to talk about being an airline pilot.

Mark's Plan

Physical Energy Outlets

Put out gym mats and small trampoline

Outdoor Explorations

Take crepe paper streamers out to measure & enjoy the wind — keep a record each day.

Focused Observations

Watch all children for vocabulary development related to airports, planes & pilots & dramatic play (how extensive, cooperative?)
Jesse - fine motor
Graham & Molly - are transitions any better?

Challenging Children's Thinking

Guessing Jar - How many M&M's do you think are in there?

	Monday	Tuesday	Wednesday	Thursday	Friday
Teacher-led Large Group Activities	"Paw Paw Patch" "Hickelty Pickelty" "One Two" Daily Routines "What do we know about airports, planes & pilots"	"Willoby Walloby" "Circle Time" "Friends" "What do we want tomorrow?" Questions for Jack's Dad	"Hello Neighbor" Jack's Dad visits	Greg & Steve Record "Space Walk" Write thank you to Jack's Dad	"Paw Paw Patch" "Hello Neighbor" Read over "Planes & Pilots" Book
Teacher-led Small Group Activities	Take photos of airport & plane dramatic play	Write book using photos & children's dictations — they write their own names	Count wheels on various transportation vehicles. Graph		Make paper airplanes

Mark's Plan

Focused Early Learning General Reflection

Date: November 17, 2009   Teacher: Susie

What Worked Well

Children loved dancing with scarves & playing balloon catch.

Much, much interest in flock of geese outside.

What Did Not Work Well

Children were not interested in cars & trucks activities. — much wandering

Individual Child Information

Cailin & Zach were first to notice geese & get lots of other children interested as well.

Talk to speech pathologist about Kelly's articulation.

Kelly's Mom had her baby!

To Consider in Future Plans

Let's do a Geese Project!

Watch Kelly — she may need extra hugs.

Susie's Reflection

The Focused Early Learning Weekly Planning Framework

Date: Nov. 19, 2006   Teacher: Susie

Child-led Exploration in the Rich Classroom Environment

Blocks Label block constructions with signs identifying what it is and the architects

Dramatic Play Act out grocery store and shopping

Manipulatives Use playdough & compare quantities; Develop fine motor skills.

Art Make eyedropper paintings & paper-strip collages; trying new expressive media

Sensory Table Wash the babydolls & manipulative toys

Library Read & listen to books about geese & ducks

Writing Center Write "letters" on stationery & envelopes to class friends.

Ongoing Projects
GEESE

Math Moments
Count the geese at the pond each day — keep a record

Scientific Inquiries
On Friday bake banana bread — observe changes in ingredients as mixed.

Reading and Writing
Help children use name cards at the writing center.

Steps to Relationship Building
Let Cailin & Zach take the lead as "Geese Watchers"

Individual Adjustments
Help Grant get to more activities by using his stander — especially the water table.

Bring in some early reader books for Martin, Emily, and Juanita.

Susie's Plan

8: Following Children's Interests with Ongoing Projects/Studies 105

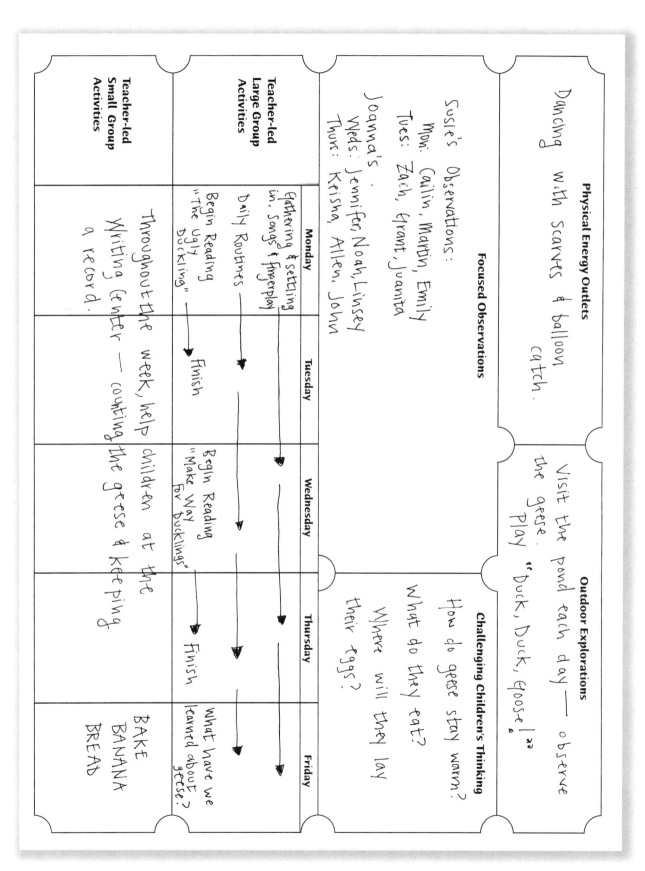

Physical Energy Outlets

Dancing with scarves & balloon catch.

Focused Observations

Susie's Observations:
- Mon: Cailin, Martin, Emily
- Tues: Zach, Grant, Juanita

Joanna's
- Weds: Jennifer, Noah, Linsey
- Thurs: Keisha, Allen, John

Outdoor Explorations

Visit the pond each day — observe the geese. Play "Duck, Duck, Goose!"

Challenging Children's Thinking

How do geese stay warm? What do they eat? Where will they lay their eggs?

	Monday	Tuesday	Wednesday	Thursday	Friday
Teacher-led Large Group Activities	Gathering & settling in, Songs & fingerplay / Daily Routines / Begin Reading "The Ugly Duckling"	→ Finish	Begin Reading "Make Way for Ducklings"	→ Finish	What have we learned about geese?
Teacher-led Small Group Activities	Throughout the week, help children at the Writing Center — counting the geese & keeping a record.				BAKE BANANA BREAD

Susie's Plan

In the bird example from Mrs. Chang's classroom, the fascination exhibited by both the children and the adults was a clue to the teachers that this was a spontaneous event worth building activities around. Because the nest building was an ongoing process that the children could directly witness, the topic had potential for in-depth learning and consideration by all in the class.

Judy Harris Helm and Lillian Katz give seven specific criteria for considering topics for in-depth classroom investigation in *Young Investigators: The Project Approach in the Early Years* (2001, 14–16). Here's what they think a good topic for investigation looks like:

1. The topic should be more concrete than abstract. It should involve lots of firsthand, direct experiences and real objects to manipulate.
2. The topic must be easily related to the children's prior experiences.
3. There should be sites nearby related to the topic so that the children can visit them as part of their investigation.
4. The topic should enable the children to do research with minimal assistance from adults.
5. The children should be able to represent what they know and learn by using skills and methods appropriate to their age such as dramatic play and construction.
6. Topics should relate to program goals.
7. Topics should be culturally relevant to the children and their families.

Using these criteria, let's analyze the bird and nest-building topic. *(See Mrs. Chang's plan on pp. 109–110.)* It provided first-hand opportunities for exploration. It was concrete and not abstract because the children could see and observe the nest-building bird and other birds everyday. Most children have seen birds in their everyday life, whether it was watching the pigeons in a city park, cardinals in the backyard trees, or ducks in an apartment house pond. Therefore, this topic related to children's prior experiences with birds. Children could represent their observations through drawing, painting, working with clay or wire, and building nests. They could write or tell stories about the birds, act out dramatizations, or make up songs. They could collect and analyze feathers and eggs, look at books of various types of birds from around the world, and read favorite fictionalized stories about birds.

Program goals could be met through all of the activities designed. Mrs. Chang's plan for the children to look at bird books in the class library is helping meet developmental goals of exploring the world around them, using books as resources, and developing vocabulary. Her provision of

Focused Early Learning General Reflection

Date: 10/02/00 Teacher: Mrs. Chang

What Worked Well

Good response to movement activities by most children

Great interest in bird building nest outside of classroom

Name recognition in pairing

What Did Not Work Well

Cooking activity took too long -- too much adult involvement rather than kids

Some throwing sand at sand table again

Need more copies of favorite books -- some fighting in class library

Individual Child Information

Sean still has difficulty following routines -- especially transitioning.

Josie Did Not Want To dance -- let her watch until she's ready

Could Susie help her? Be her friend?

To Consider in Future Plans

Add Bird activities to classroom

Supervise sand more carefully? change materials?

Mrs. Chang's Reflection Week 1

Focused Early Learning General Reflection

Date: 10/9/00 Teacher: Mrs. Chang

What Worked Well

The children were constant in their viewing of the nest-building process.

The binoculars + kind call tape were hits!

Some beautiful feather collages were created.

What Did Not Work Well

Our nest materials did not hold together very well and children lost interest.

Should we split a large group time into 2 smaller group times?

Individual Child Information

Jenna is our bird expert — very knowledgable — from a bird-watching family

Some children still painted + built as usual — Sam, Nathan, Angie

Jessica were not as interested in birds.

To Consider in Future Plans

Make toilet paper tube binoculars?

Go on a bird watching walk?

Do some egg activities?

Put bird seed in sensory table?

Mrs. Chang's Reflection Week 2

The Focused Early Learning Weekly Planning Framework

Date: 10/12/00   Teacher: Mrs. Chang

Child-led Exploration in the Rich Classroom Environment

Blocks
Construct & build with blocks, cars, trucks & traffic signs

Dramatic Play
Imitate family life & tasks

Manipulatives
Complete puzzles with varying number of pieces

Reading and Writing
Make cards with names of birds — put at writing center.

Art
Make toilet paper tube binoculars

Sensory Table
Pour & measure bird seed

Library
Study books & magazines about birds; listen to bird call tapes

Writing Center
Make a bird book with stickers

Ongoing Projects
Birds & nests (week 2)

Math Moments
Keep record on bird walk of birds seen. Graph when we return

Scientific Inquiries
Experiments with children about eggs: raw, whipped, hard boiled, scrambled, soft boiled, fried

Steps to Relationship Building
Invite any family "bird expert" to come in & share or go on our bird walk.

Individual Adjustments
Let Jenna lead discussions at group time. Encourage Sam, Nathan, Angie & Jessica's interests — but don't force.

Mrs. Chang's Plan Week 3

Physical Energy Outlets

Walking, tiptoeing, hopping the ABC & number rings.

Outdoor Explorations

Look for birds every day. Thursday - bird walk.

Focused Observations

Jenna - Vocabulary
Children who try to figure out our bird - what we their problem solving strategies?

Nick & Josh - attention span any longer?

Challenging Children's Thinking

Who can figure out by looking in our bird books what kind of bird is building her nest outside our classroom? Is her call on our bird tape?

	Monday	Tuesday	Wednesday	Thursday	Friday
Teacher-led Large Group Activities	"Mine We Are Together" "Way up in the Sky" Daily Routines Read "Are You My Mother?"	"Did you Ever see a Lassie" "Here's a Baby Bird" → Read "Chickens Aren't the only Ones"	"If you have on Red" "Way up in the Sky" → Read "The Best Nest"	"Mine we are Together" "Here's a Baby Bird" Children Choose a favorite book	"Chickea Chickea" "Hello Neighbor" → Write a group story about our bird walk
Teacher-led Small Group Activities	Throughout the week, Sylvia will invite children to practice fine motor skills by cutting out pictures in magazines, picking up buttons & toothpicks with tweezers, and using hole punches.				

Mrs. Chang's Plan Week 3

feathers to make feather collages helps children develop creativity by using expressive media and focusing on the observable and tangible aspects of objects. Reading bird stories and singing and acting out songs about birds helps develop listening and comprehension skills and provide children with opportunities to develop dramatic play and rhythmic movement. The topic of birds is appropriate for all cultures as it is part of the human experience of nature, and offers opportunities for the children to discuss the place of birds in their home cultures. Some families may have birds as pets, or raise chickens for eggs. Other parents or relatives may hunt grouse or ducks. This spontaneous event provided a good topic for study according to these criteria.

What would a bad topic be? In many classrooms, teachers have traditionally coordinated curriculum around certain themes and topics that changed each week. In fact, some programs publish their week-by-week themes up to three years in advance! Such weekly themes are not what I am recommending here. Often, they do not meet the criteria that Helm and Katz have set out because such pre-determined topics are not in response to children's interests, and are not chosen because of a specific event the children are witnessing (like the nest-building bird). Instead, they are chosen because the teacher likes the activities she has organized around the topic, or she has been told she must "cover" certain topics in order to please a supervisor or the parents of the children. The fallacy here is that the various topics for projects or studies are the source of curriculum. *Curriculum is not the list of topics or projects teachers do across the year.* Preschool curriculum is focused on children's development—the strategies they are using to learn more about their world and the skills they are developing to observe, talk about, and represent what they are learning with a variety of materials. And they are asked to do this in a classroom that has other children with whom they have to get along. No matter what the theme or topic, these same goals (and more: fine and gross motor, early math and reading, and so on) are the focus. The theme or topic is a way to engage the children—to capture their interest and develop their attention, to make learning fun and enjoyable so that the all-important developmental goals are continually being worked on.

Let's use the criteria from Helm and Katz to analyze some of the topics that are often chosen for these pre-determined themes. First of all, let's look at a week of activities devoted to "bears." In most locations, children cannot have direct, firsthand experiences with bears. Instead, videos and photographs must be used, which moves us away from concrete rather than abstract presentation. For a preschooler, a Pokemon video is just as "real" as a video about bears. If a community has a zoo to visit, children could see bears, but that one visit would provide the only opportunity for direct experience. The exception might be if the school was located somewhere like Anchorage, Alaska, or Churchill, Manitoba, where bears wandering through town are part of everyday life. If children cannot have real life experiences with bears, they cannot as easily investigate and research the topic in a meaningful, hands-on way so important to the preschool age group. They cannot as easily represent their learning through dramatic play, creativity, and construction because they do not have as much understanding to express through these activities.

Let's contrast the bear topic above to a study of children's favorite stuffed animals, which would include teddy bears, of course! Now, the topic is much more concrete and can involve many firsthand experiences and real objects to manipulate, study, research, compare, play with, and discuss. Children can represent their learning in a variety of ways, sorting and categorizing their stuffed animals, comparing and contrasting types of fur, sizes, and amount of loving by the owner. They can stage puppet shows with stuffed animals, and listen to and read books like *Corduroy* and *Teddy Bear's Picnic*. Chants like "Teddy Bear, Teddy Bear, Turn Around" relate directly to the topic at hand and help children develop program goals of following directions and using positional words. Most importantly, the children are interested and engaged in such a topic because it relates so directly to their daily lives. Their favorite stuffed animal is a dear friend who provides them comfort when they are sad or scared. Learning more about the stuffed animals of their friends may hold their interest far more than dealing with the abstract of polar bears in the Arctic or grizzly bears in the wild.

Some other topics that do not meet the criteria include: snow and winter in a warm weather climate (or in a cold-weather climate when no snow has fallen!); ocean for children in a landlocked state, or even a town far away from the beach; far-away countries and cultures to which no children in the class have any ties; historical holiday stories, given that young children are unsure of the meaning of "yesterday," "today," and "tomorrow," let alone several hundred years ago.

What are some topics that do meet the criteria, then? Anything to do with the child and his or her everyday life, such as: my body, my family, what I like to eat, my mom's and dad's jobs, my feelings. Preschoolers are at a very egocentric age and will relish projects that relate directly to them. All of these topics can easily be explored firsthand, and learning about them can be investigated and represented by the children in a variety of ways. Again, remember, it is not necessary to coordinate every activity in the classroom to a topic! Don't rack your brains trying to come up with

Diana: *"I always ask myself—'Why am I doing this study or theme? What are my goals for the children?' If I don't have solid, developmental goals in mind—if my answer to myself is 'Because it's cute. I've got lots of cute activities to tie to it'—I know that I'm going down the wrong path because I've learned over my years of teaching that those are the topics that really don't interest the kids as much. I don't see the same kind of engagement I see when I choose one that really taps into their life experiences."*

materials in every area that relate. Instead, plan for activities that are meaningful and make sense. The rest of the classroom environment will stand as the rich and inviting place that it is.

Other topics include anything in nature that can be experienced firsthand: weather and seasonal traits of your area; classroom and/or household pets; animals, insects, and plants that can be directly experienced and observed outdoors (preferably right on your playground and school grounds); local natural attractions. If you live near water, study it! I met a teacher once whose town is near a large cave. Guess what? She studied caves with the children very successfully. That wouldn't be possible in many other areas, would it? Many machines and mechanical objects interest children. Special celebrations and events in your area can also be a source of good project topics. I live in Indianapolis where, with our Indianapolis 500 and other car races, many preschool programs explore racing—a very important part of our community. Programs in rural California may study the rodeo, while those on the Navajo reservation in New Mexico focus on many activities around the corn harvest, including making "kneel down bread" and celebrating with the Corn Dance. Such topics would not be appropriate in urban settings around the country where studies of tall buildings, subway systems, or city parades might be more appropriate.

How often do you change topics or initiate a project? There is no need to change a topic of study each week unless the children lose interest that quickly. In fact, there is no set time period for any topic. As we pointed out in chapter 3, if you have set up the classroom environment to be rich and inviting, with a variety of materials in each learning area, exploring the classroom can be the focus for long periods of time, and can be returned to as the focus throughout the year.

Change or end a topic or project when the children are no longer as engaged or interested. You can use the criteria for changing the setup of the classroom, or the materials that are present, to decide when to change a project as well.

- The children are not choosing to work on the project, or in areas of the classroom devoted to the project.
- The children are bored with the topic (they may say they are bored; they may appear bored in activities relating to the project; or they may change the related activities themselves).
- The children's behavior is not productive or positive when they are working on the project.
- Another topic of interest has emerged in the classroom and is engaging the attention of some or all of the children.

Children may show an emerging interest by using materials in new ways. They may organize all of the food in the dramatic play area into a store and pretend to buy and sell to one another. Changing activities then to relate to a grocery store, planning a field trip to a grocery store, and adding materials, stories, and songs related to this important family experience would be warranted.

Sometimes, the determining factor for a project or study is a field trip or a special site visit. This may not arise specifically from the children's interests. Rather, it is planned by the teacher (often well in advance in order to arrange transportation and parent helpers) because she knows the focus of the visit will be of interest to the children and may very well lead to ongoing investigations and project work.

The preschool program where Sharon taught was located on a high-school campus. So, Sharon went and talked with the auto shop teacher, asking if he thought a visit to his shop would be appropriate for her young children. He was willing to take the safety precautions necessary and enthusiastic about sharing his students' work with Sharon's. The visit was a roaring success and children's involvement in a variety of activities related to repairing cars went on for a long period in Sharon's classroom.

How long does one keep planning with a topic in mind? Again, a teacher has to be carefully observing the children and assessing their ongoing interest and engagement in the topic. Barbara had noticed that her children were using the stuffed animals and stethoscopes to play veterinarian's office in the dramatic play area. She decided to respond by providing materials and activities to follow up on that interest. The children acted out caring for the animals for three to four weeks. They read books about veterinarians, visited a veterinarian's office, practiced giving the animals shots, and bandaged their legs. One day, Barbara noticed that the children had packed up all of the veterinarian's equipment and turned the dramatic play area back into a house and kitchen. She knew then that her project was over. She changed the focus of her planning back to exploring the classroom environment, and watched to see what new topics might emerge as the children used the learning areas to their fullest.

Being flexible like all of these teachers helps the topics or projects truly follow children's interests. Using the criteria outlined above helps teachers remember that the best projects are those that can be directly experienced by the children and relate to their lives.

> **Diana:** *"Most of my topics last three to four weeks. In my newsletter, I tell the parents that I've planned for certain themes and activities, but I also tell them 'Don't hold me to it! I never know exactly what direction we'll go and what the children's interest might be.' Since my program is located on my farm, things happen every day related to the farm animals and machinery that might change the focus of our activities."*

chapter 9

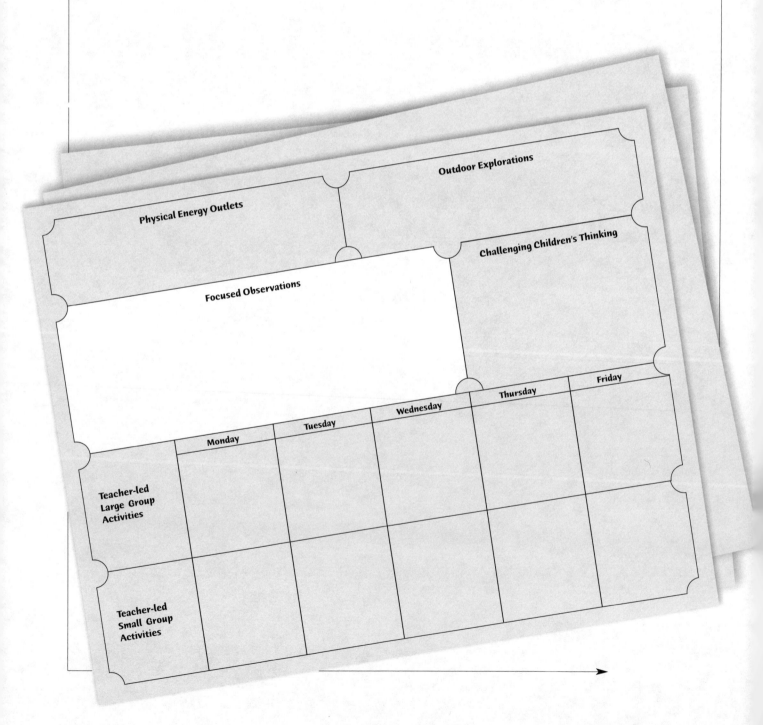

Focused Observations and Assessing Children's Learning

teachers are constantly observing the children in their classroom. However, they don't always write down or document what they observe, which must become a habit in order to overcome that little problem most of us have—poor memory!

When I am in a classroom, I feel like my brain is a video camera in constant action. Even though I'm not writing down everything that I see, I am taking it in mentally. And, it often comes back to visit me later in the day, that night, or even in my dreams. Sometimes, my video camera brain takes in so much information that I feel overwhelmed. Many teachers talk about observing their children but not being sure exactly what they should be looking for. They see so much that they must filter through their recollections to figure out what was important, and plan responses and interventions with particular children.

Focused Observations

Focused observations can help with this process. The planning framework includes a box to identify the focus for observations. If your focus will be on specific children for each staff member each day, here's where that list can be written. If your focus will be on specific classroom areas or activities for each teaching colleague, you will note that here. And, if your focus will be on a specific developmental learning goal, such as those listed above, you will note that in this portion of the framework.

Sometimes teachers divide up the children in the classroom and each observes the same group of children over time, perhaps with attention to a specific developmental goal each week. Or each teacher may focus instead on a specific area of the classroom, again paying attention to a specific developmental task. You and your colleagues will need to communicate clearly about this aspect of your teaching. Recording it on the planning framework will give it importance—almost as if you've been given an assignment. The assignments can be given in reflection meetings as you discuss what you saw the children doing and who needs to be observed next.

Here are some examples of how teachers have written their focused observations on the planning framework.

Valerie: *"Sometimes I write in the Focused Observations section something like, 'will be observing two students during work time to see how they interact with their peers.' I keep doing this so that every week my assistant and I focus on two different students. Other times, I write something focused to a certain goal like, 'matching—comprehension responses to vocabulary taught.'"*

Focused Observations

Linde: Monday - Willie, Luis, Stephanie
　　　 Tuesday - Gregory, Michelle, Anna
　　　 Weds. - Tony, Alicia, Albert
　　　 Thurs - Jon, Missy, Megan
Sofia: Mon - Jon, Missy, Megan
　　　 Tues - Tony, Alicia, Albert
　　　 Wed - Gregory, Michelle, Anna
　　　 Thurs - Willy, Luis, Stephanie

Linde's Plan

Focused Observations

YESENIA - BEHAVIOR   PAYING ATTENTION
ERIK - CUTTING   COUNTING
VANESSA - WRITING & DRAWING
DEREK - RECOGNIZING NAMES, SHAPES & COLORS

Mark's Plan

Focused Observations

FOCUS ON FINE MOTOR SKILLS AS
CHILDREN TRACE AND DRAW

Darlene's Plan

Focused Observations

Glenna: Supervise art with paper maché
Debbie: Float
Both observe specifically for language development

Glenna and Debbie's Plan

Mary: *"I like the observation section as well. I've been using it to make notes about what I need to observe or what kind of observations I'm looking for."*

Focus on Teaching: Writing Down Your Observations

If teachers are using the reflection framework on a daily basis, some observations could be written directly in the Focused Observations box. As the teaching team discusses the day and comments on things they saw and heard the children do, one member can be recording that discussion on the reflection framework. Here's an example.

Focused Observations

> Jessica drew a person; used right handed fist grip with marker; head with arms coming out of sides all by herself; said, "It's me!" even had her curly hair.
>
> Juan finished 2 puzzles with a little help from teacher Lydia – each had 10–12 pieces. He turned pieces around & around until they fit.

Gayle's Reflection

The framework doesn't have a lot of room for observations, especially more extensive ones that would include quotes from the child and other details. It is not necessary to write observations on the frameworks. Many teachers prefer to have clipboards placed around the classroom with note paper or sticky pads and pens. Using a method that works for you is most important in getting observations written down. A portfolio process that includes written observations will be introduced later in this chapter.

Valerie: *"Since my children are identified with special needs, I incorporate their IEP goals into my 'Focused Observations' and then use the reflection about the results of those observations for my progress reports."*

Identifying Children to Observe

By identifying specific children to observe, teachers can make sure that no child is missed. Many teaching teams split up the class list into several small groups for observation purposes. Then each teacher or teaching assistant focuses their eyes and ears more closely on four to five children a day. The workload of observing all the children is shared. Different adults often see different things in the children's behavior and performance.

Many programs assign primary caregivers to children so that one teacher really gets to know each child fully and can be the main contact with the family. If that's the case, the primary caregiver should be the one to observe his or her assigned children. Teaching colleagues who see the child in action, then, report to the child's primary caregiver so that information is shared and observations are noted.

Focusing observations on specific children each day helps teachers get a well-rounded picture of what that child can do, and what that child may struggle with. Without focus, the children who have more problems with other children often take center stage. They need adult intervention, which they receive in order to protect other children and to help them learn self-control. However, if teachers only focus on those children, so many others will be missed. The picture that will arise about these more needy children will be lopsided toward their negative behavior.

Some children ask for lots of attention—not for negative behavior, but for positive interaction with the teacher they know and love. Again, it's easy to focus on these children because they ask for it. The ones who are often missed are the children who don't ask for negative or positive attention. They can easily become invisible unless some intentional action is taken to make sure that they are being observed as well.

Observing Specific Areas of the Classroom

Focusing observations can also mean paying attention to specific areas of the classroom. Again, many teaching colleagues will identify specific locations where they will spend their time just for the purpose of gaining information about the children in a variety of activities. This can be a very effective plan for providing adult supervision during activity time or learning center time. In Glenna's classroom, Glenna and her assistant, Debbie, would discuss where they were needed most during the time the children were involved in independent work at the learning areas. Some weeks, both of them would "float," as they called it. This meant that they were not assigned to any specific area; rather, they moved around the classroom and helped the children as needed. Were new materials necessary to keep a group interested in the manipulatives area? Did the children in blocks need help making more space between their ever-expanding construction and the block shelves? Did a child need a lap to sit on and read a book in the library? Had the paint spilled at the easel?

In the weeks when Glenna and Debbie both "floated," they were each available to solve various problems, provide support to the children, and, most important, observe the children in action in a variety of activities. They each carried a clipboard with a class list on it, a sticky note pad, and a pen or pencil. That way, they could quickly note what they saw the children do, and make a check mark next to the child's name as they documented their observation. The class list helped them to remember to observe all the children, even those not asking for direct attention.

One thing the two of them always kept in mind, however, was that they should try to avoid ending up in the same corner of the room. They tried to distance themselves in such a way that one or the other could see all parts of the classroom. This provided safety and communicated to the children that the adults were ready to help them when problems arose.

Not always did both Glenna and Debbie float. Some weeks, they planned an art activity that needed close monitoring. Some weeks, it was a cooking activity or a small group learning task that required attention. In those cases, one of them was assigned to a specific area, and the other was the floater. This again helped to focus observations. If Glenna was leading a small group on shape and color recognition, she could easily note each child's knowledge on a clipboard with a list of the children's names on it. If Debbie was cooking with the children, she may have been focusing her observations on their abilities to follow directions or their fine motor skills when handling small measuring spoons and eggbeaters.

> **Pam:** *"My teaching assistants and I could determine who would watch specific children each week, as well as if we would watch for any developmental areas in particular."*

Other Times of Day to Focus Observations

Circle time, snack time, and outdoor play are also ripe with opportunities for teaching colleagues to focus their observations on different aspects of the activity involved. At circle time, if one colleague is reading a story, the other can note which children are following along with the print, which are comprehending the story and making predictions, and which don't seem to have a clue. At snack time, sitting at different tables allows each teacher to interact with different children. Vocabulary can easily be noted as friendly conversation occurs among the children and adults. Outdoors, one team member can be posted near the highest climbing structure to provide safety. The other can float around to other areas of the playground and keep an eye on safety concerns elsewhere. The two teachers' observations will be different in focus then. The one by the climber will probably see more evidence of risk taking (or lack of risk taking) and problem solving as the children wait in line to climb the slide. The floater may see more gross-motor skills such as running and jumping, and learn more about the children's interests in nature and weather. (Again, don't forget to take that clipboard, sticky pad, and pen outdoors with you!)

Observing for Developmental Goals

Focusing observations can also mean paying particular attention to different aspects of the children's development and learning. In Pam's inclusive preschool classroom, she and her assistants often identify a developmental area on which they will focus for a week or two. Their observations will be exclusively about that area. For example, one week they may concentrate on the children's growing language skills. Another week, they may focus on fine motor development. In this way, their assessment of each child's growth and learning is well-rounded rather than skewed to only behavior, or only motor or cognitive skills.

When teachers do not focus observations by specific learning or developmental areas, some of those areas may very well be missed. Every teacher has favorite things to do with the children. Some of us are more artistic. Some of us are mathematical. Some of us really like to help children develop self-control. If we focus only on the areas that appeal to us, we'll lose that picture of the whole child. Instead, we have to force ourselves to think about all areas of development and learning.

Here are two ways to analyze what you tend to focus on when watching children. If you have observations already written down, read through them. As you do so, ask yourself honestly: "What is the primary focus of this observation? Is it behavior and social/emotional development? Is it cognitive learning? Is it language? Is it creative development, or reading and writing? Is it fine or gross motor?" With each observation, make a tally mark next to each of these developmental categories. Did you tend to have more observations in one than in the others?

Here's another way to evaluate yourself. Look over the following list of developmental learning areas. Then, rank order this list placing a number one by the area you really think you pay the most attention to (or like the best in your teaching practice), a number two by your second choice, and so on. Look over your ranking. More than likely you focus your observations much more on your first, second, and third choices and much less on your less favorite ones.

Developmental Learning Areas
- __ Social/emotional development
- __ Language development
- __ Fine motor development
- __ Gross motor development
- __ Cognitive development (thinking, problem solving, math skills)
- __ Reading and writing development
- __ Creative development

In my conversations with teachers, many will admit that they tend to observe with greater intensity in the social/emotional area. Language is another area teachers of young children tend to focus on. And, both are important for good reason! Young children are learning how to function with groups of other children and adults, often away from their homes for the first time. Their language development is exploding in ways that are astonishing and exciting to witness. However, if we only focus on social/emotional and language development, we miss so much else about a child's accomplishments, strengths, and weaknesses. Focusing our observations to make sure that we are paying attention to all areas will give us a far more detailed, accurate, and complete picture of each child's unique capabilities.

Assessing Children's Learning

The integration of curriculum planning with assessment of children's learning is the key to good teaching. Therefore, implementing assessment processes that will help with the planning process is essential. And, focusing observations is part of the process of authentically assessing each child's progress and development.

In our book, *Focused Portfolios™: A Complete Assessment for the Young Child* (2001), Bev Engel and I show you how to organize focused observations of children's growth and tie those observations to developmental milestones. This portfolio design meshes beautifully with the Focused Early Learning planning and reflection frameworks.

The Focused Portfolios™ process asks teachers to observe children and document those observations in factual, descriptive anecdotes, or observation notes. Special forms are provided on which to record the anecdotes with all of the pertinent information about the child, his or her age, the observer's name, and the date of the observation. A photograph of the child in action, or a work sample that the child produced, can accompany the anecdote. Or the anecdote can stand alone as the documentation of the child's performance. Additional information is then included on the portfolio form—information that identifies exactly what developmental or learning information the teacher sees as significant in this observation. For example, an anecdote that includes direct quotes from the child may serve as evidence of the child's growing language abilities. The teacher then notes right on the portfolio collection form what specific language skills the child has that this observation demonstrates.

The anecdotes or observation notes, written for assessment purposes, are factual descriptions of what the child did and/or what the child said. They are not evaluative or judgmental. Instead, the teacher continually edits herself as she writes, making sure that the words noted only describe the child's actions or quote the child's utterances. There is no place for opinion or interpretation in this part of the assessment process. This is the collection of evidence or documentation to make later judgments and evaluations in summarizing reports and family/teacher conferences.

Here are some examples of completed Focused Portfolios™ developmental milestones collection forms with focused teacher observations on the children's accomplishments.

Coordinating the Focused Portfolios™ Assessment with the Focused Early Learning Frameworks

Because the basis for the Focused Portfolios™ assessment is observation of children in action, the planning framework helps a teacher to identify which children will be observed each week. This happens in the "Focused Observations" portion of the plan. Also, there are other sections on the planning form that may involve thinking about individual children and their capabilities and needs. The "Steps to Relationship Building" and "Challenging Children's Thinking" boxes can both be sources of individualized information about specific children. Assessment is ongoing during the reflection process as teachers think back to the children's accomplishments, problems, challenges, and next steps.

In chapters 3 and 5, more goal-oriented plans were shown both for the learning areas in the classroom environment, and for integrating academics and developmental learning throughout all activities. The goals chosen by a teacher for these plans do not come out of thin air. Instead, they should be carefully considered and reflect the best thinking about child development from the early childhood education field.

The goals set out in Focused Portfolios™ are adapted directly from NAEYC's *Developmentally Appropriate Practice in Early Childhood Programs*, revised edition (Bredekamp and Copple 1997). In the Focused Portfolios™ they are formatted into developmental milestones charts that go across age groups from birth to five years. When using the planning framework, teachers could turn directly to these charts to insert specific developmental milestones as the goals for various activities. This is especially useful in the following areas on the framework: Child-Led Exploration in the Rich Classroom Environment; Steps to Relationship Building; Reading and Writing; Math Moments; Scientific Inquiries; Physical Energy Outlets; Outdoor Explorations: Challenges; and Teacher-Led Large and Small Group Activities.

Whether or not you use the Focused Portfolios™ assessment approach, teachers can turn to one of the other developmental checklists available

Developmental Milestones Collection Form
Version #1 Preschooler

Child's Name _Nicholas_   Age _4_
Observer _Maria_   Date _4/16/99_

Check off the *areas of development* that apply:

- ☐ Thinking, Reasoning & Problem-Solving
- ☑ Emotional and Social Competency
- ☐ Gross-Motor Development
- ☐ Fine-Motor Development
- ☐ Language and Communication
- ☐ Reading & Writing Development
- ☐ Creative Development

This photo, work sample and/or anecdote illustrates the following *developmental milestone(s)*:

Can sense a person's feelings and has some ideas how to help.

Check off whatever applies to the context of this observation:

- ☑ Child-initiated activity
- ☐ Teacher-initiated activity
- ☐ New task for this child
- ☑ Familiar task for this child
- ☐ Done independently
- ☐ Done with adult guidance
- ☑ Done with peer(s)
- ☑ Time spent (1-5 mins.)
- ☐ Time spent (5-15 mins.)
- ☐ Time spent (15+ mins.)

Anecdotal Note: Describe what you saw the child do and/or heard the child say.

Jessica and Darianne were fighting over the dolls. Nicholas saw them fighting. He picked up the extra doll and tried to hand it to Darianne. I heard him say "Darianne you can have this one."

© 2001 Gaye Gronlund and Bev Engel. May be reproduced for classroom use only.

Portfolio Collection Form (Nicholas)

Developmental Milestones Collection Form
Version #1 Preschooler

Child's Name __Linsey__ Age __3 yrs. 8 mos.__
Observer __Beth__ Date __10-21-98__

Check off the *areas of development* that apply:

- ❏ Thinking, Reasoning & Problem-Solving
- ❏ Emotional and Social Competency
- ❏ Gross-Motor Development
- ❏ Fine-Motor Development
- ❏ Language and Communication
- ❏ Reading & Writing Development
- ☒ Creative Development

This photo, work sample and/or anecdote illustrates the following *developmental milestone(s)*.

__explores a variety of expressive media__

Check off whatever applies to the context of this observation:

- ❏ Child-initiated activity
- ☒ Teacher-initiated activity
- ❏ New task for this child
- ☒ Familiar task for this child
- ☒ Done independently
- ❏ Done with adult guidance
- ❏ Done with peer(s)
- ☒ Time spent (1-5 mins.)
- ❏ Time spent (5-15 mins.)
- ❏ Time spent (15+ mins.)

Anecdotal Note: Describe what you saw the child do and/or heard the child say.

We had just read a book, "Dem Bones," and talked about our bones and body parts. Linsey began to paint a skeleton — then when her neighbor left, she took his brush. She continued to paint with 2 brushes at once and said, "My Mom and Dad are dancing."

© 2001 Gaye Gronlund and Bev Engel. May be reproduced for classroom use only.

Portfolio Collection Form (Linsey)

and use their specific developmental accomplishments as the source for goal setting on the planning framework.

On pp. 129–130 are some examples of using the developmental milestones charts in *Focused Portfolios*™ as a source for goals for various areas of the planning framework. The broad area of development is included in parenthesis after the specific developmental milestone or goal.

In observing children at work in all of these activities, teachers gain knowledge of the progress the children are making towards these developmental goals. Teachers can decide which specific goals are appropriate for their children, and how many to include on the planning framework. The above example may be too overloaded for some. Use your judgment on how many goals to include in your own planning.

Combining Reflection and Curriculum Planning with Assessment

When the reflection process is included with the planning framework, teachers are able to review observations and coordinate their planning, continually reevaluating how their curricular activities are contributing to each child's growth and development. All of this information is important to the assessment process. Combining the Focused Portfolios™ process with the Focused Early Learning Frameworks will help teachers see the connections between their room arrangement and activity planning, and the progress the children make. The portfolios will be the evidence of that progress.

On pp. 131–134 are some examples of reflections a teacher made about individual children, accompanied by the portfolio pieces documenting those reflections and observations.

Using Other Assessment Tools with the Frameworks

If a program is using a different type of observational assessment tool, the planning framework can still be tied-in. Focusing observations, writing factual and descriptive anecdotes, and using some reference to developmental standards (such as these familiar preschool checklists—Creative Curriculum® Developmental Continuum, the High/Scope® Child Observation Record, or the Work Sampling System®) will still fit beautifully with the planning and reflection process for a truly individualized curriculum. Many states have written early childhood standards for their preschool programs. A source such as this for goal-setting and assessment purposes can easily be integrated into the Focused Early Learning Frameworks.

Valerie: *"The Focused Early Learning Frameworks state everything that I'm doing and show how I'm incorporating the Illinois Early Learning Standards throughout all of my activities. Now, I'm going to start collecting portfolio items using the Focused Portfolios™ process related to our state standards. That will tie it all together!"*

The Focused Early Learning Weekly Planning Framework

Date: _____ Teacher: _____

Child-Led Exploration in the Rich Classroom Environment

Blocks
Build simple to complex block structures (fine motor)

Dramatic Play
Listen to others & participate in conversations (language)

Manipulatives
Count objects & refer to quantity of items (thinking, reasoning & problem-solving)

Reading and Writing
Listen to stories read aloud, asking questions (reading-writing)

Art
Begin to name person, place or things in drawings (creative)

Ongoing Projects
Explore the world around them (thinking, reasoning & problem-solving)

Math Moments
Approach new tasks & solve problems through observation & trial & error (thinking, reasoning & problem-solving)

Sensory Table
Begin to willingly take turns (social-emotional)

Library
Play at reading by reading the pictures (reading-writing)

Writing Center
Print first name (fine motor)

Scientific Inquiries
Focus on the observable & tangible aspects of objects & events (thinking, reasoning & problem-solving)

Steps to Relationship Building
Show comfort with new people & situations (social-emotional)

Individual Adjustments
Work hard to use language to express feelings (social-emotional)

Weekly Planning Framework with NAEYC goals

Physical Energy Outlets

CAN BALANCE & CLIMB

(GROSS MOTOR)

Outdoor Explorations

WALK, RUN, TURN & STOP WELL

(GROSS MOTOR)

Focused Observations

Challenging Children's Thinking

BEGIN TO GENERATE IDEAS & SUGGESTIONS FOR PROBLEM-SOLVING

(THINKING, REASONING & PROBLEM-SOLVING)

	Monday	Tuesday	Wednesday	Thursday	Friday
Teacher-led Large Group Activities	LEARN WORDS TO SIMPLE FINGERPLAYS, RHYMES & SONGS (LANGUAGE)				
	IS CURIOUS ABOUT LETTERS, WORDS & SOME CONVENTIONS OF PRINT (READING - WRITING)				
Teacher-led Small Group Activities	CAN FOLLOW MULTI-STEP INSTRUCTIONS (LANGUAGE)				

Plan with NAEYC goals

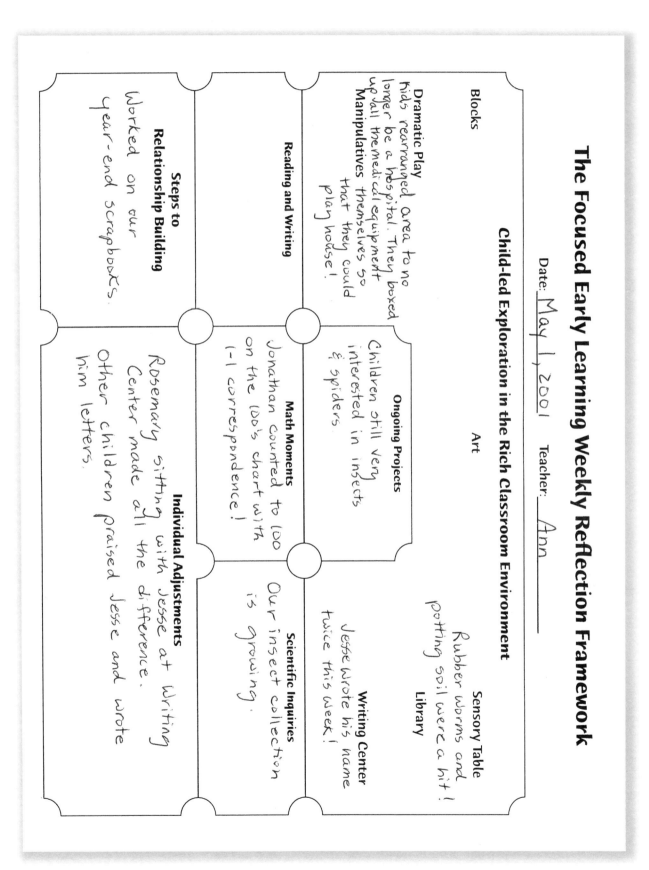

The Focused Early Learning Weekly Reflection Framework

Date: May 1, 2001   Teacher: Ann

Child-led Exploration in the Rich Classroom Environment

Blocks

Dramatic Play
kids rearranged area to no longer be a hospital. They boxed up all the medical equipment

Manipulatives
Manipulatives themselves so that they could play house!

Art

Sensory Table
Rubber worms and potting soil were a hit!

Library

Ongoing Projects

Reading and Writing

Math Moments
Jonathan counted to 100 on the 100's chart with 1-1 correspondence!

Ongoing Projects
Children still very interested in insects & spiders

Scientific Inquiries
Our insect collection is growing.

Writing Center
Jesse wrote his name twice this week!

Individual Adjustments

Steps to Relationship Building
Worked on our year-end scrapbooks

Individual Adjustments
Rosemary sitting with Jesse at Writing Center made all the difference. Other children praised Jesse and wrote him letters.

Ann's Reflection

Ann's Plan

Physical Energy Outlets

Outdoor Explorations

The outdoor Bug Hunt would have been more successful with more magnifying glasses. We need to borrow more.

Focused Observations

Challenging Children's Thinking

Jonathan took the "How many bugs can you count?" challenge - counted to 100!

	Monday	Tuesday	Wednesday	Thursday	Friday
Teacher-led Large Group Activities		We could read "Hungry Caterpillar" and "Grouchy Ladybug" every day!			
Teacher-led Small Group Activities	Need to be sure to get Germaine, Michael, Tracie, and Sasha to small group next week. Their absences don't help.				

Developmental Milestones Collection Form
Version #1 Preschooler

Child's Name **Jesse**   Age **4.8**
Observer **Ann & Rosemary**   Date **April 30, 2001**

Check off the *areas of development* that apply:

- ☐ Thinking, Reasoning & Problem-Solving
- ☐ Emotional and Social Competency
- ☐ Gross-Motor Development
- ☒ Fine-Motor Development
- ☐ Language and Communication
- ☒ Reading & Writing Development
- ☐ Creative Development

This photo, work sample and/or anecdote illustrates the following *developmental milestone(s)*:

Prints 1st name
is curious about letters, words & some conventions of print

Check off whatever applies to the context of this observation:

- ☐ Child-initiated activity
- ☒ Teacher-initiated activity
- ☒ New task for this child
- ☐ Familiar task for this child
- ☐ Done independently
- ☒ Done with adult guidance
- ☐ Done with peer(s)
- ☐ Time spent (1–5 mins.)
- ☒ Time spent (5–15 mins.)
- ☐ Time spent (15+ mins.)

Anecdotal Note: Describe what you saw the child do and/or heard the child say.

Rosemary invited Jesse to come to the Writing Center with her on 2 separate days this week. He easily found his name card. Rosemary helped him trace the letters on his card both with his finger and with a fat pencil. Jesse initially held the pencil in a fist grasp. Rosemary corrected his grasp and his writing became much more readable. He smiled broadly and showed everyone in the room how he had written his name!

© 2001 Gaye Gronlund and Bev Engel. May be reproduced for classroom use only.

Portfolio Collection Form (Jesse)

Developmental Milestones Collection Form
Version #1 Preschooler

Child's Name __Jonathan__ Age __5.1__
Observer __Rosemary__ Date __April 28, 2001__

Check off the *areas of development* that apply:

- ☒ Thinking, Reasoning & Problem-Solving
- ☐ Emotional and Social Competency
- ☐ Gross-Motor Development
- ☐ Fine-Motor Development
- ☐ Language and Communication
- ☐ Reading & Writing Development
- ☐ Creative Development

This photo, work sample and/or anecdote illustrates the following *developmental milestone(s)*:

Counts objects and refers to the quantity of items

Check off whatever applies to the context of this observation:

- ☒ Child-initiated activity
- ☒ Teacher-initiated activity
- ☐ New task for this child
- ☒ Familiar task for this child
- ☒ Done independently
- ☐ Done with adult guidance
- ☐ Done with peer(s)
- ☐ Time spent (1–5 mins.)
- ☐ Time spent (5–15 mins.)
- ☒ Time spent (15+ mins.)

Anecdotal Note: Describe what you saw the child do and/or heard the child say.

A challenge was offered to the children this week: "How many bugs (rubber) can you count?" Jonathan got out the 100's posterboard chart and carefully placed one bug on each number, counting aloud until he had reached 100. His naming of the numbers was correct. We have never heard him count this high before.

© 2001 Gaye Gronlund and Bev Engel. May be reproduced for classroom use only.

Portfolio Collection Form (Jonathan)

Making observation and documentation a regular part of every classroom day and identifying who on the teaching team will focus their observations on which children are essential steps to making Focused Portfolios™ or other observational assessments work well. Learning to write factual and descriptive anecdotes that only include information about what the child did and/or said but that do not include teacher judgments or interpretation is another critical factor in using these approaches to assessment.

The Individual Child Web

The assessment process is about teachers getting to know each child very well so that they can plan learning opportunities that match the capabilities and needs of each one. The Individual Child Web, which appears on the next page, has been designed to encompass the various aspects of children that can impact their success in an early childhood program. As a teacher gets to know a child, she fills in information she gains on the web. She records the results of relationship building steps with each child. By the end of the program year, as all areas have been completed, she has a full and rich picture of this young individual in his care.

Some of the information on the web is obtained in initial interviews with the family. Many programs have intake sheets that are filled out by family members as part of the registration process. Some programs interview the parents as the children are registered. In either case, many of the aspects on the Individual Child Web can be addressed at that time.

Other parts of the web will become evident as the child attends regularly and teachers get to know him. All of the teachers involved should be continually discussing what they are learning about this child, and reflecting upon the categories listed on the web. Many programs identify a primary caregiver for each child. She may be the one who is responsible for recording on the web the information about the child gained from the family, and from the reflection of the teaching staff. At the very least, it's a good idea to assign one person as the primary record keeper for each child. This ensures that this important job will be taken care of.

How Often to Work with the Individual Child Web

The web design gives a broad picture of the child's overall development. Therefore, it does not need to be used daily or weekly. Some teachers use it three times a year when they are meeting with family members: first, in a get-acquainted or intake meeting; second and third, in preparation for family/teacher conferences.

Pam: *"We use Focused Portfolios™ as our assessment tool. The frameworks fit nicely with the portfolios."*

Mary: *"Connecting my planning, reflection, and portfolio assessment is working well for me."*

Vicki: *"I've been using Focused Portfolios for two years now—this assessment process is truly in my heart. It is so child and family friendly. Now, I'll combine it with the planning and reflection frameworks."*

Individual Child Web

- Family
- Developmental Strengths
- Emerging Developmental Areas
- Physical Needs and Health Issues
- Life Experiences
- **Child**
- Emotional Make-Up
- Culture
- Learning Style
- Interests
- Dispositions to Learning and Response to Challenges

Teachers have found that showing the web to the parents in the first meeting lets them know that you will be working hard to find out exactly who their child is, and the best ways to make the preschool experience successful for him. The parents can then give you family information, cultural background, information about the child's life experiences, and physical needs and health issues. You can ask for their take on their child's developmental strengths, interests, learning styles, emotional makeup, emerging developmental areas, dispositions to learning, and response to challenges. Families have a wealth of information to help give teachers a sense of the child. The web provides a way to invite their input and structure the conversation at this important getting-acquainted time.

On pp. 138–139 are some examples of individual child webs filled out in the intake process with families.

Revisiting the Individual Child Web before each family/teacher conference allows the teacher to review the family's comments at the beginning of the preschool year, and compare what he has learned about the child over several months in the preschool classroom. He can corroborate what the parents told him, and add information. The Individual Child Web can guide the writing of a summary report about the child's progress and the next steps planned to stimulate and enhance this child's development. It can then be included in the portfolio presentation to the family.

On pp. 140–141 are some examples of the same completed Individual Child Webs from above with additional comments from the teacher added before the first family/teacher conference.

On pp. 142–143 are some examples of those same webs with the end of year comments from the teacher before the final family/teacher conference. Notice how much more complete the information is. These teachers really know their children, don't they?

The information written on the final child webs is the result of a full year of careful planning and reflection. The Focused Early Learning frameworks help teachers to represent the integration of the very best curricular approaches they are using every day in the classroom to address the needs and learning traits of preschool children. An incredible number of accommodations for individual children occur in the life of a successful preschool classroom. The frameworks, in combination with the Individual Child Web, will help teachers develop an ongoing record of the ways that they integrate their own knowledge of child development with the specific needs and interests of the children they teach.

Individual Child Web

Child: Colin

*Intake 9/7/01

Family
- Mom, Dad, baby sister (Gwen)

Developmental Strengths
- Loves being read to — listens to several books in a row.

Emerging Developmental Areas
- Not very interested in alphabet.

Physical Needs and Health Issues
- Lots of ear infections — tubes in ears. Sleeps, eats well.

Life Experiences
- Travels, been to museums, zoo, etc.

Emotional Make-Up
- Gets frustrated — throws things

Culture
- Caucasian with Swedish + English background.

Learning Style

Interests
- Cars, trucks, super heroes, music.

Dispositions to Learning and Response to Challenges

Colin's Web—Intake

9: Focused Observations and Assessing Children's Learning 139

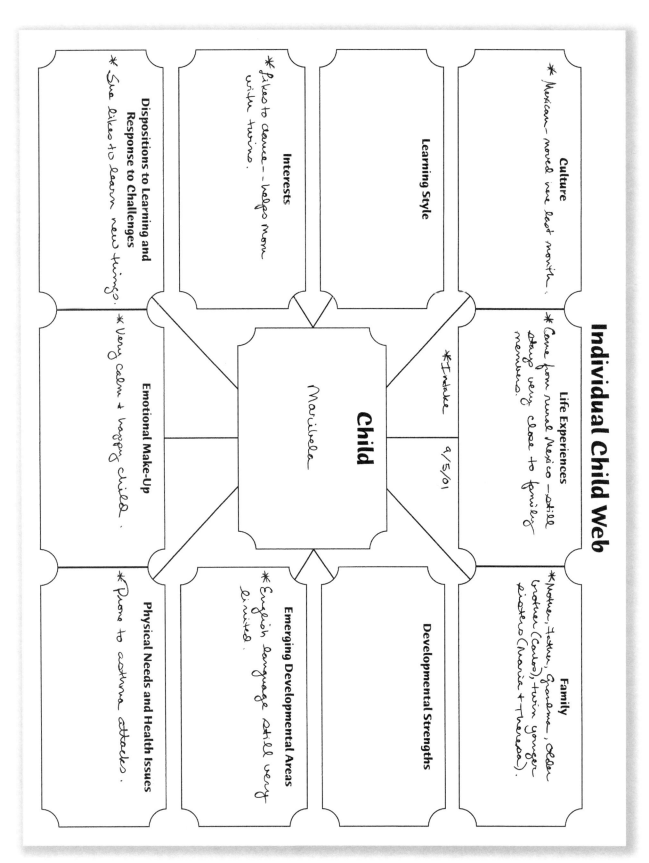

Maribela's Web—Intake

Individual Child Web

Family
- ★ Mom, Dad, baby sister (Gwen)
- ○ Loves his baby sister!

Developmental Strengths
- ★ Loves being read to — listens to several books in a row.
- ○ Can tell whole stories, great block & lego builder.

Emerging Developmental Areas
- ★ Not very interested in alphabet.
- ○ Writes part of his name.

Physical Needs and Health Issues
- ★ Lots of ear infections — tubes in ears. Sleeps, eats well.
- ○ Hearing?

Life Experiences
- ★ Traveled, been to museums, zoo, etc.
- ○ Went to Toronto with his family — told us all about it.

★ Intake 9/7/01
○ Conference 11/3/01

Child
Colin

Emotional Make-Up
- ★ Gets frustrated — throws things.
- ○ Very independent.

Culture
- ★ Caucasian with Swedish + English background.

Learning Style
- ○ Prefers physical movement, hands-on trial + error himself.

Interests
- ★ Cars, trucks, superheroes, music.
- ○ Dinosaurs, whales

Dispositions to Learning and Response to Challenges
- ○ Likes to do his own thing rather than join group but is productively engaged.

Colin's Web—First Conference

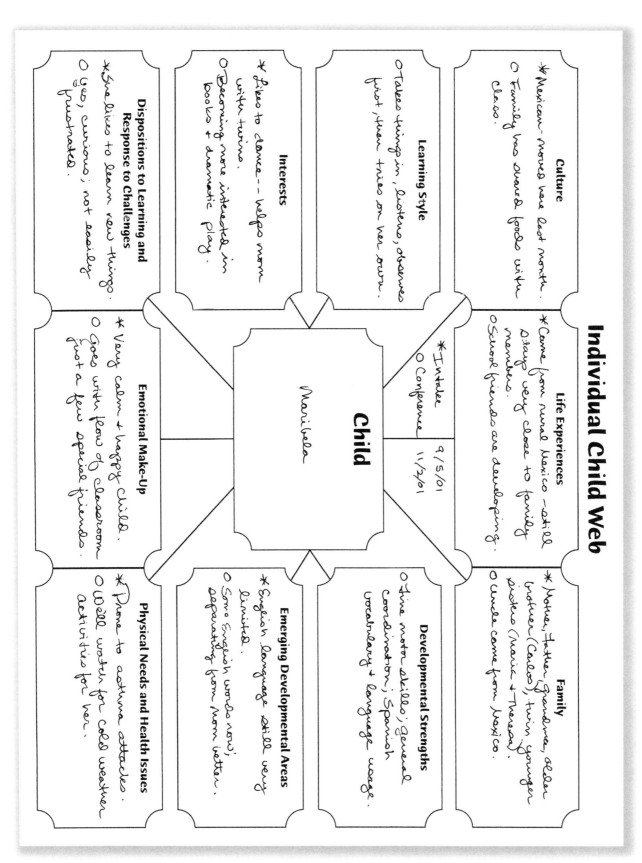

Maribela's Web—First Conference

142 Focused Early Learning

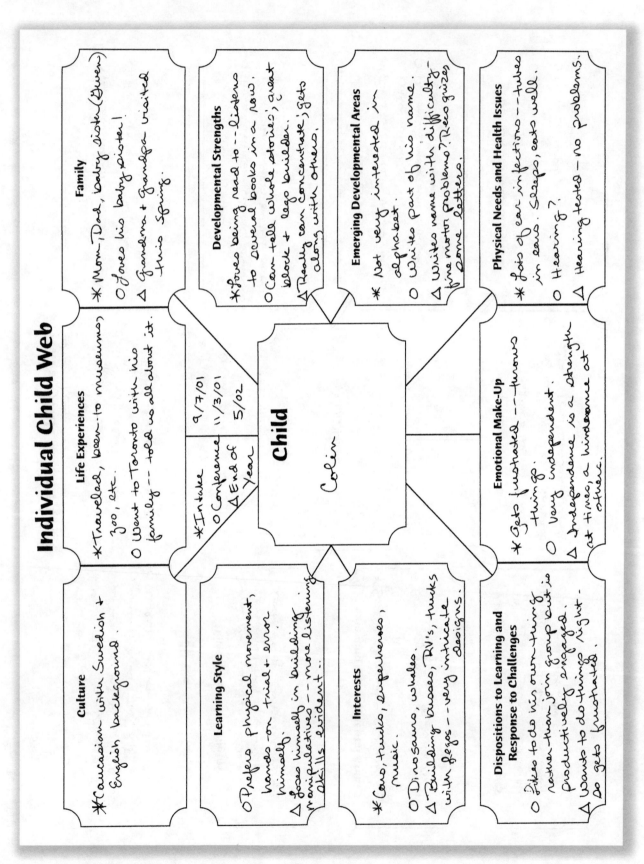

Colin's Web—Final Conference

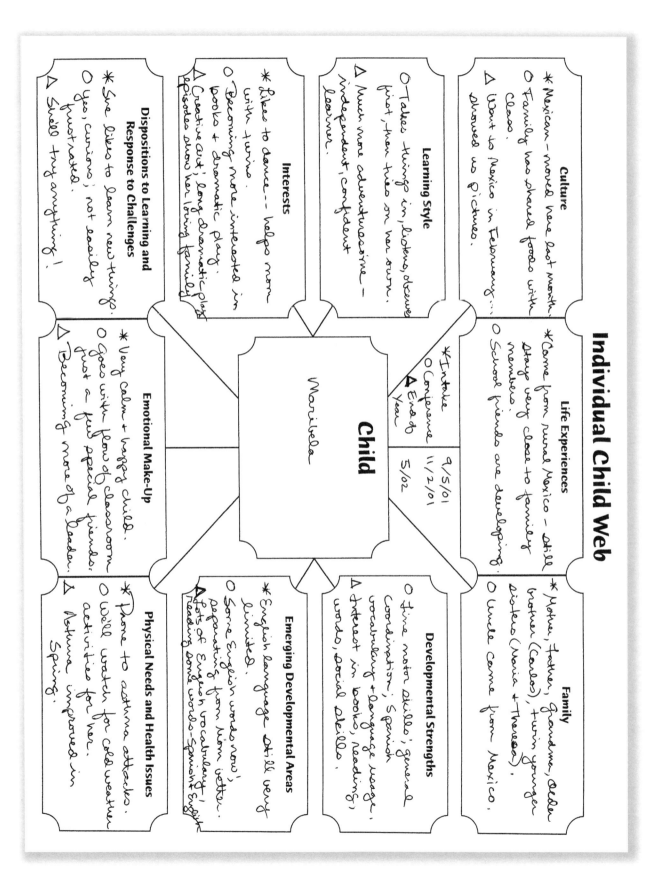

Maribela's Web—Final Conference

appendixes

The Focused Early Learning Weekly Planning Framework

Date: _____ Teacher: _____

Child-led Exploration in the Rich Classroom Environment

- Blocks
- Dramatic Play
- Manipulatives
- Art
- Ongoing Projects
- Math Moments
- Sensory Table
- Library
- Writing Center
- Scientific Inquiries

Reading and Writing

Steps to Relationship Building

Individual Adjustments

Appendix A:
Focused Early Learning Forms

Forms on the following pages may be reproduced.

Included are the following:

- The Focused Early Learning Weekly Planning Framework
- The Focused Early Learning Weekly Reflection Framework
- Focused Early Learning General Reflection
- Individual Adjustments Form
- My Own Weekly Planning Framework
- My Own Weekly Reflection Framework
- Individual Child Web

The Focused Early Learning Weekly Planning Framework

Date: _____ Teacher: _____

Child-led Exploration in the Rich Classroom Environment

- Blocks
- Dramatic Play
- Manipulatives
- Sensory Table
- Art
- Library
- Writing Center

Ongoing Projects

- Reading and Writing
- Math Moments
- Scientific Inquiries

Steps to Relationship Building

Individual Adjustments

© 2003 Gaye Gronlund. May be reproduced for classroom use only

	Monday	Tuesday	Wednesday	Thursday	Friday
Teacher-led Large Group Activities					
Teacher-led Small Group Activities					

Physical Energy Outlets

Focused Observations

Outdoor Explorations

Challenging Children's Thinking

© 2003 Gaye Gronlund. May be reproduced for classroom use only.

The Focused Early Learning Weekly Reflection Framework

Date: _____ Teacher: _____

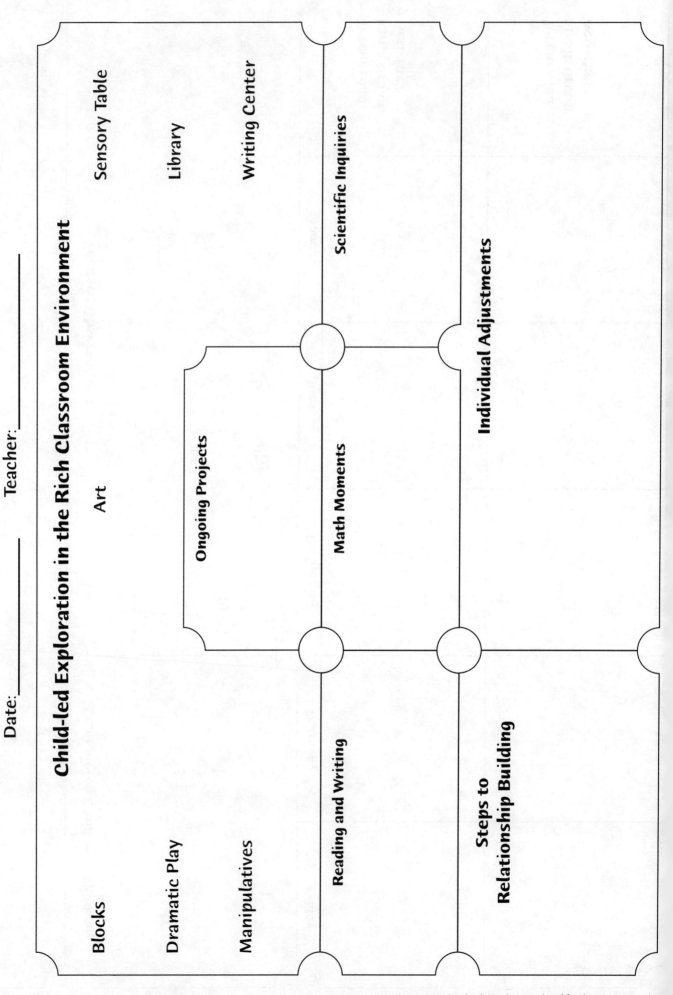

Child-led Exploration in the Rich Classroom Environment

- Blocks
- Dramatic Play
- Manipulatives
- Art
- Sensory Table
- Library
- Writing Center

Ongoing Projects

Reading and Writing
Math Moments
Scientific Inquiries

Steps to Relationship Building
Individual Adjustments

© 2003 Gaye Gronlund. May be reproduced for classroom use only.

	Monday	Tuesday	Wednesday	Thursday	Friday
Teacher-led Large Group Activities					
Teacher-led Small Group Activities					

Physical Energy Outlets

Focused Observations

Outdoor Explorations

Challenging Children's Thinking

© 2003 Gaye Gronlund. May be reproduced for classroom use only.

Focused Early Learning General Reflection

Date: _____ Teacher: _____

What Worked Well	What Did Not Work Well

Individual Child Information	To Consider in Future Plans

© 2003 Gaye Gronlund. May be reproduced for classroom use only

Individual Adjustments

For Week of: _____ Teacher: _____

Child's Name	Planned Adjustment	Child's Name	Planned Adjustment

© 2003 Gaye Gronlund. May be reproduced for classroom use only.

My Own Weekly Planning Framework

Date: _____   Teacher: _____

Child-led Exploration in the Rich Classroom Environment

Blocks

Dramatic Play

Manipulatives

Art

Sensory Table

Library

Writing Center

© 2003 Gaye Gronlund. May be reproduced for classroom use only.

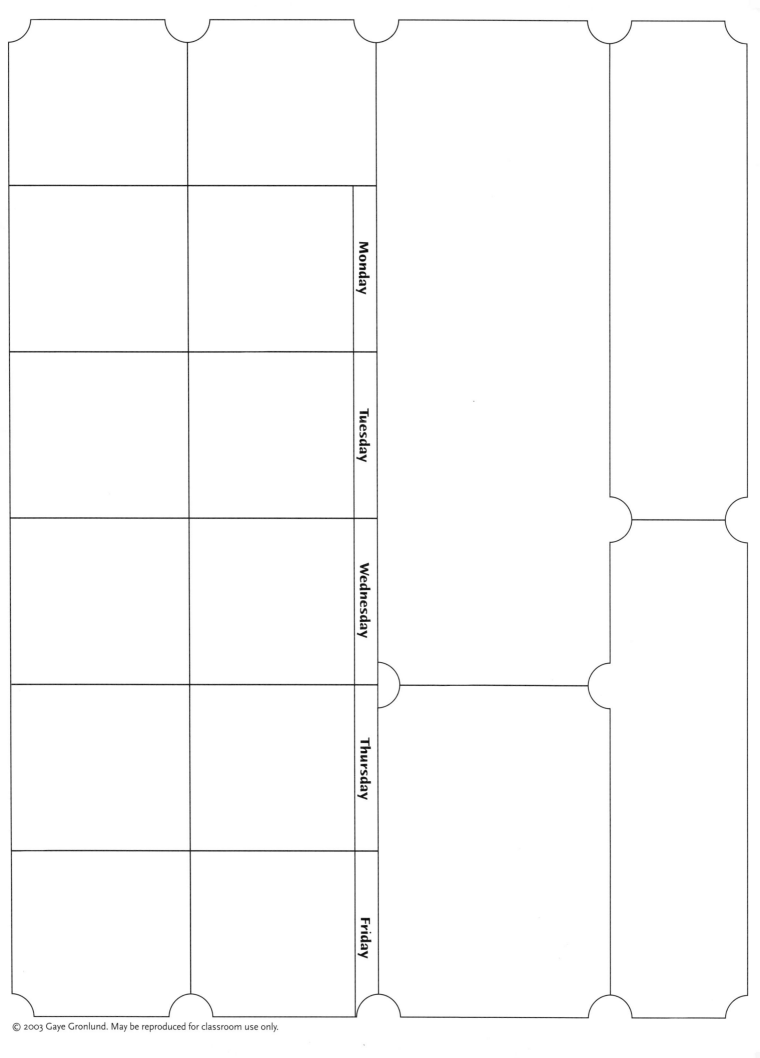

© 2003 Gaye Gronlund. May be reproduced for classroom use only.

My Own Weekly Reflection Framework

Date: _____ Teacher: _____

Child-led Exploration in the Rich Classroom Environment

- Blocks
- Dramatic Play
- Manipulatives
- Art
- Sensory Table
- Library
- Writing Center

© 2003 Gaye Gronlund. May be reproduced for classroom use only.

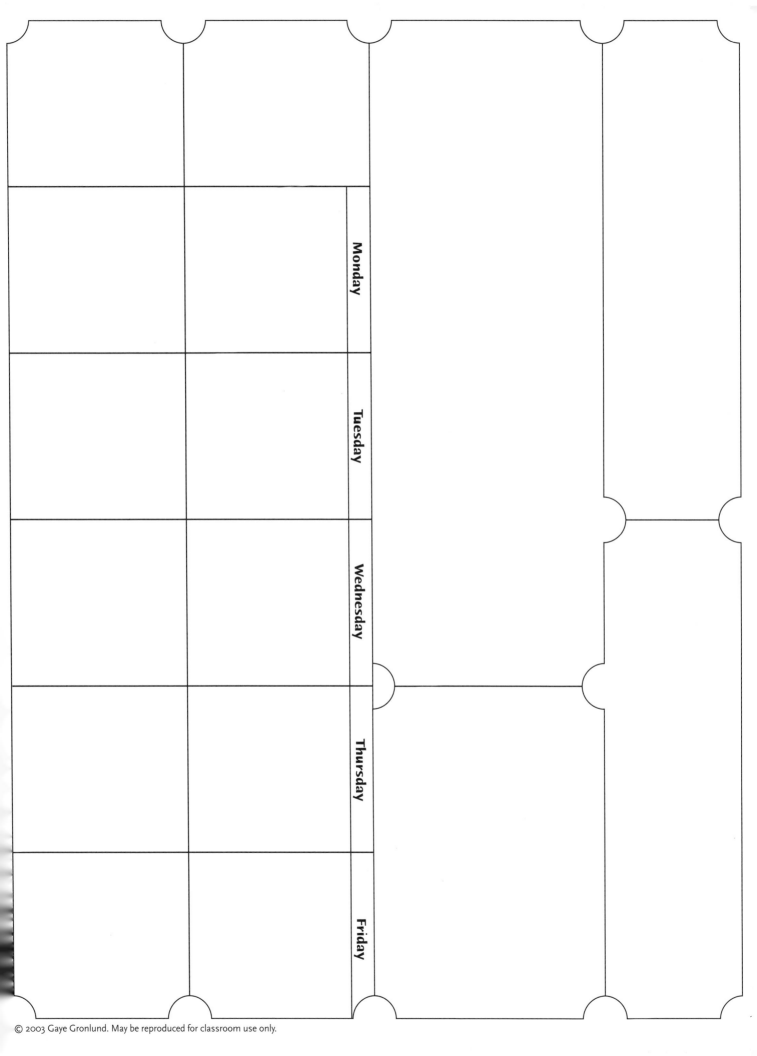

© 2003 Gaye Gronlund. May be reproduced for classroom use only.

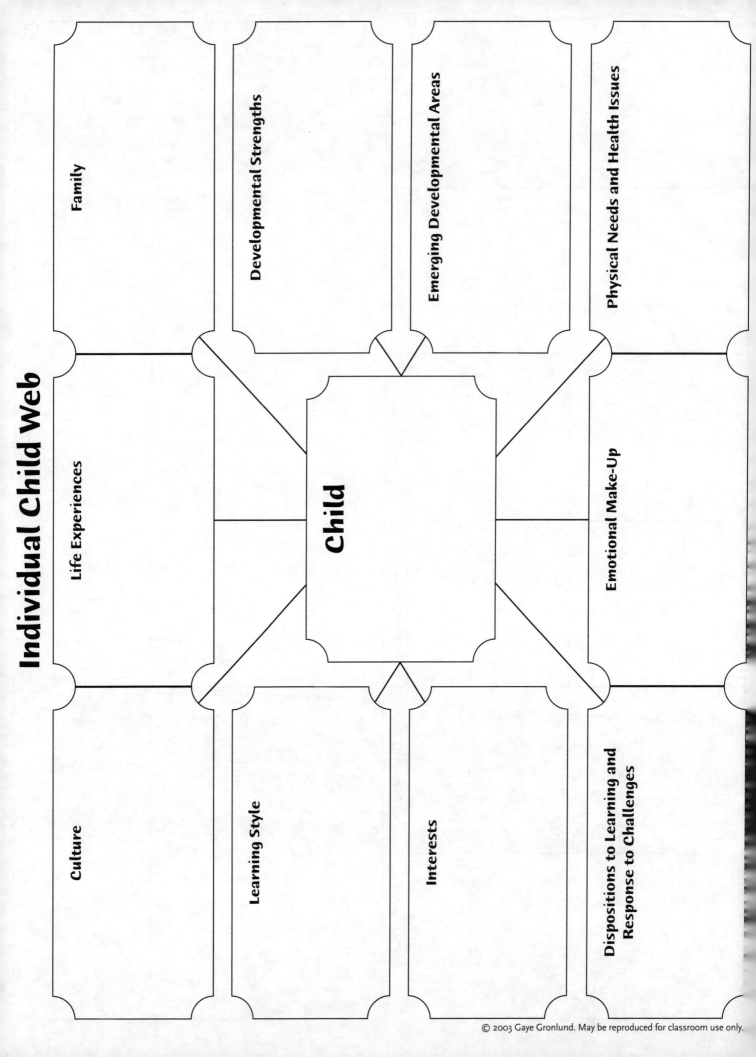

Appendix B: References

Ashton-Warner, Sylvia. 1963. *Teacher.* New York: Simon & Schuster.

Bredekamp, Sue, and Carol Copple, eds. 1997. *Developmentally appropriate practice in early childhood programs.* Rev. ed. Washington, D.C.: National Association for the Education of Young Children (NAEYC).

Carter, Margie, and Deb Curtis. 2003. *Designs for living and learning.* St. Paul: Redleaf Press.

Curtis, Deb, and Margie Carter. 1996. *Reflecting children's lives: A handbook for planning child-centered curriculum.* St. Paul: Redleaf Press.

Daniels, Ellen R., and Kay Stafford. 1999. *Creating inclusive classrooms.* Washington, D.C.: Children's Resources International, Inc.

Dodge, Diane Trister, Laura J. Colker, and Cate Heroman. 2002. *The Creative Curriculum® for preschool.* 4th ed. Washington, D.C.: Teaching Strategies.

Gould, Patti, and Joyce Sullivan. 1999. *The inclusive early childhood classroom: Easy ways to adapt learning centers for all children.* Beltsville, Md.: Gryphon House.

Gronlund, Gaye, and Bev Engel. 2001. *Focused Portfolios™: A complete assessment for the young child.* St. Paul: Redleaf Press.

Hayes, Kathleen, and Renee Creange. 2001. *Classroom routines that really work for pre-k and kindergarten.* New York: Scholastic.

Helm, Judy Harris, and Lilian G. Katz. 2001. *Young investigators: The project approach in the early years.* New York: Teachers College Press.

Jones, Elizabeth, and John Nimmo. 1994. *Emergent curriculum.* Washington, D.C.: NAEYC.

Jones, Elizabeth, with Elizabeth Prescott. 1984. *Dimensions of teaching-learning environments: A handbook for teachers in elementary schools and day care centers.* Pasadena, Calif.: Pacific Oaks College.

USA Today. 2000. Pablum preschools cheat young learners, 20 October.

York, Stacey. 1998. *Big as life: The everyday inclusive curriculum.* 2 vols. St. Paul: Redleaf Press.

Index

A

academic and developmental learning
    "Challenging Children's Thinking" box, 60–62
    developmentally appropriate programs, 3–4
    Erickson's stages in development, 43
    in everyday classroom activities, 57
    importance of, 66
    observations of, 122–128, 133–134
    planning framework, 58–59
    reflection framework, 59
    "university course catalog" approach, 62–66
accommodations, as key component of curriculum, 2, 6–8. *See also* individual adjustments
activities
    goals for, 8
    length of, 7
    outdoor exploration, 75–76
    physical energy outlets, 72, 77–78
    See also teacher-directed activities; themes
adjustments, as key component of curriculum, 2, 6–8. *See also* individual adjustments
airplane theme, 99–102
art, learning area for, 26–27, 37
Ashton-Warner, Sylvia, 85
assessment
    planning framework, 128, 129–130
    portfolio approach, 124–128, 133–134
    reflection framework, 128, 131–132
    as small group activity, 83
    web approach, 135–143, 158

B

bear theme, 111–112
bird theme, 33–35, 98, 106–111
blocks, 26–27, 37, 63
breathing in/out activities, 85–87, 88
Bredekamp, Sue, 125

C

"calling to" songs, 92–93
Carter, Margie, 38, 40
"Challenging Children's Thinking" box, 60–62
chants, 92–94
"Chickee Chickee," 92
child development. *See* academic and developmental learning
choice time
    classroom environment strategies, 89–91
    vs. teacher-directed activities, 7, 81–82, 85–87, 91
circle (group) time, 82–84, 87–89, 122
"Circle Time" song, 94
"Clap, Clap, Clap," 94
classroom environment
    for academic growth, 62–63
    choice time strategies, 89–91
    evaluation of, 38–40
    floor plan example, 37
    as key component of curriculum, 4, 5
    planning framework, 15, 26–28
    reflection framework, 28–35
    for teaching facilitation, 35–38
cognitive development, 123
communication, with families, 54–55
conferences, 54, 137
confidentiality issues, of weekly plan posting, 21, 53
cooperative games, 77–78
Copple, Carol, 125
"Cows and Ducks," 77–78
Creative Curriculum® Developmental Continuum, 128
creative development, 123
curriculum
    approaches focused on children's interests, 97–98, 100
    assessment tools, 128
    five key components, 2–8
    vs. topics, 111
    See also academic and developmental learning
Curtis, Deb, 38, 40

D

daily schedules, 64–65, 70, 85–87
development. *See* academic and developmental learning
Developmentally Appropriate Practice in Early Childhood Programs (Bredekamp and Copple), 125
developmentally appropriate practices, vii
Dimensions of Teaching-Learning Environments (Jones and Prescott), 38
discipline, 90
dramatic play, 26–27, 37

E

emergent curriculum, 97, 100
Emergent Curriculum (Jones and Nimmo), 100
Engel, Bev, 124
equipment. *See* materials and equipment
Erikson, Erik, 43, 81
evaluations, 38–40. *See also* assessment
exercise
    outdoor explorations, 73–77, 122
    physical energy outlets, 7, 70–73, 85–87

F

families, 44, 54–55, 137
fine motor development, 123
finger play, 92–94
floor plans, 37
Focused Early Learning Frameworks, viii, 11–12. *See also* planning framework; reflection framework
focused observations
    for assessment, 124–128
    identification of children for, 120–121
    importance of recording, 117
    methods, 120–124
    planning framework, 118–119, 125
    reflection framework, 16, 120
Focused Portfolios™, 124–128, 133–134
forms, reproducible, 147–158
frameworks, viii, 11–12. *See also* planning framework; reflection framework
free choice time. *See* choice time
"Friends," 94

G

games, 72, 76, 77–78
general reflection form, 19, 20, 152
goals, 8, 26–28, 30
goose theme, 100, 103–105
gross motor development, 123
group area in classroom, 37
group time, 82–84, 87–89, 122

H

"Hello Neighbor," 94
Helm, Judy Harris, 106
"Help," 78
"Hicklety Picklety," 92
High/Scope® Child Observation Record, 128

I

IEPs (Individual Education Plans), teachers' comments on, 52, 53, 120
"If You Have on Red," 93
individual adjustments
    challenges to thinking, 60, 62
    examples of, 49–53
    form, 153
    frequency guidelines, 53–54
    reflection framework, 16
    for relationship building, 47–48
Individual Child Web, 135–143, 158
Individual Education Plans (IEPs), teachers' comments on, 52, 53, 120
interests of children, activities focused on, 8, 97–100

J

Jones, Elizabeth (Betty), 38, 100

K

Katz, Lilian, 106
"Knee to Knee," 78

L

language arts, 63–64
language development, 123–124
large group time, 82, 84, 87–89
learning, as key component of curriculum, 2, 3–4. *See also* academic and developmental learning
learning areas. *See* classroom environment
lesson plans. *See* planning framework
libraries, 26–27, 37, 66

M

manipulatives, 26–27, 37
materials and equipment
    evaluation of, 38–40
    outdoor exploration, 75
    physical energy outlets, 71–72
    and relationship building, 48
    resources for, 36
    when to change, 6, 27–28, 32–35
math, 57, 58, 63–64
"The More We Get Together," 93
music, 88–89, 92–94
"Musical Chairs," 78
"My Thumbs Go Up," 93

N

National Association for the Education of Young Children (NAEYC), 3, 125
Nimmo, John, 100

O

observation, as key component of curriculum, 2, 5–6. *See also* focused observations
"One, Two," 93
ongoing projects
    focused on children's interests, 97–98
    planning framework, 98, 101–102, 104–105, 109–110
    reflection framework, 99–100, 103, 107–108
    topics for, 100, 106, 111–114
open door policy, 54
outdoor explorations, 73–77, 122

P

parents, 44, 54–55, 137
"Paw Paw Patch," 92
personality (children's), and relationship building, 52
physical energy outlets, 7, 70–73, 85–87
planning framework
    academic and developmental learning, 58–59
    assessment, 128, 129–130
    cautions about public posting of, 53
    classroom environment, 15, 26–28
    customization of, 21
    focused observations, 118–119, 125
    forms, 13–14, 148–149, 154–155
    group time, 82, 83, 84
    individual adjustments, 47–54
    ongoing projects, 98, 101–102, 104–105, 109–110
    outdoor explorations, 73–74
    overview of, 12–15
    physical energy outlets, 70–71
    relationship building, 15, 44, 45–47, 49–51
play-based programs, 62
portfolios, 124–128, 133–134
posting of weekly plans, cautions about, 21, 53
Prescott, Liz, 38
Project Approach, 97
projects. *See* ongoing projects

Q

"quieting children down" songs, 93–94

R

reading, 58, 123
recess, 73–77, 122
Reflecting Children's Lives: A Handbook for Planning Child-Centered Curriculum (Curtis and Carter), 38
reflection, as key component of curriculum, 2, 5–6

reflection framework
    academic and developmental learning, 59
    assessment, 128, 131–132
    classroom environment, 28–35
    focused observations, 16, 120
    forms, 17–18, 20, 150–152, 156–157
    group time, 84
    important areas for use of, 16
    individual adjustments, 16, 47–54
    ongoing projects, 99–100, 103, 107–108
    overview of, 15–20
    physical energy outlets/outdoor exploration, 76–77
    relationship building, 16, 45–46, 48–51
Reggio Emilia, 97
relationship building
    and child development, 43
    with families, 44, 54–55
    individual adjustments, 47–54
    as key component of curriculum, 5
    planning framework, 15, 44, 45–47, 49–51
    reflection framework, 16, 45–46, 48–51
    steps for, 44–47
"Rich and Chocolaty," 92
rich classroom environment. *See* classroom environment
risk-taking, encouragement of, 5
room arrangement, 36–37. *See also* classroom environment

S

schedules, 64–65, 70, 85–87
science, 58–59, 63, 66
"sending away" songs, 92–93
sensory tables, 26–27, 37
small group time, 83, 84
snack time, 122
social/emotional development, 123–124
social studies, 63–64
songs, 88–89, 92–94
supervision needs, and reflection framework, 29

T

Teacher (Ashton-Warner), 85
teacher-directed activities
    vs. child choice time, 7, 81–82, 85–87, 89–91
    group time, 82–84, 87–89
teacher/family conferences, 54, 137
themes
    changing, 113–114
    and children's interests, 8, 98, 99–100
    choosing, 100, 106, 111–113
thinking, challenges to, 60–62
traffic flow, 36
transitions, songs for, 88–89, 92–94
transportation theme, 99–102
trust. *See* relationship building

U

"Under the Spreading Chestnut Tree," 94
"university course catalog" approach, 62–66
USA Today, 3

W

water/sand tables, 26–27, 37
web assessment approach, 135–143, 158
weekly planning framework. *See* planning framework
"Wiggles," 93
"Willoughby Wallaby Woo," 92
Work Sampling System®, 128
writing, 58, 123
writing centers, 26–27, 37

Y

Young Investigators: The Project Approach in the Early Years (Helm and Katz), 106

Other Resources from Redleaf Press

Focused Portfolios™: A Complete Assessment for the Young Child
by Gaye Gronlund and Bev Engel
Offers an innovative way to accurately document children's growth and development by observing them in the midst of their everyday activities. Especially designed for inclusive classrooms.

Designs for Living and Learning: Transforming Early Childhood Environments
by Deb Curtis and Margie Carter
Drawing inspiration from a variety of approaches—from Waldorf to Montessori to Reggio to Greenman, Prescott, and Olds—*Designs for Living and Learning* outlines hundreds of ways to create healthy and inviting physical, social, and emotional environments for children in child care.

The Art of Awareness: How Observation Can Transform Your Teaching
by Deb Curtis and Margie Carter
Do more than watch children—*be* with children. Covering different aspects of children's lives and how to observe them, as well as tips for gathering and preparing documentation, *The Art of Awareness* is an inspiring look at how to see the children in your care—and how to see what they see.

Reflecting Children's Lives: A Handbook for Planning Child-Centered Curriculum
by Deb Curtis and Margie Carter
Keep children and childhood at the center of your curriculum and rethink ideas about scheduling, observation, play, materials, space, and emergent themes with these original approaches.

What the Kids Said Today: Using Classroom Conversations to Become a Better Teacher
by Daniel Gartrell
Contains 145 stories that explore how teachers can use conversations with children to build skills such as acceptance, cooperation, creative and peaceful problem solving, and appropriate emotional expression.

Lessons from Turtle Island: Native Curriculum in Early Childhood Classrooms
by Guy W. Jones and Sally Moomaw
The first complete guide to exploring Native American issues with children. Includes five cross-cultural themes—Children, Home, Families, Community, and the Environment.

800-423-8309
www.redleafpress.org